What Was I Thinking!

A MEMOIR IN ESSAYS

Cheryl Welch

WP
PUBLISHING

WelchDesignPublishing.com

A quick note about the photos used in this book: They have been taken over many decades using Brownie, Polaroid, 35mm, Instamatic, Disposable, Digital, and mobile phone cameras. The resulting prints have been handled and scratched and are sometimes bent and blurry. However, they remain nothing short of magic in their existence and in the love they represent.

I HOLD MY BREATH, QUIET MY INTRUSION

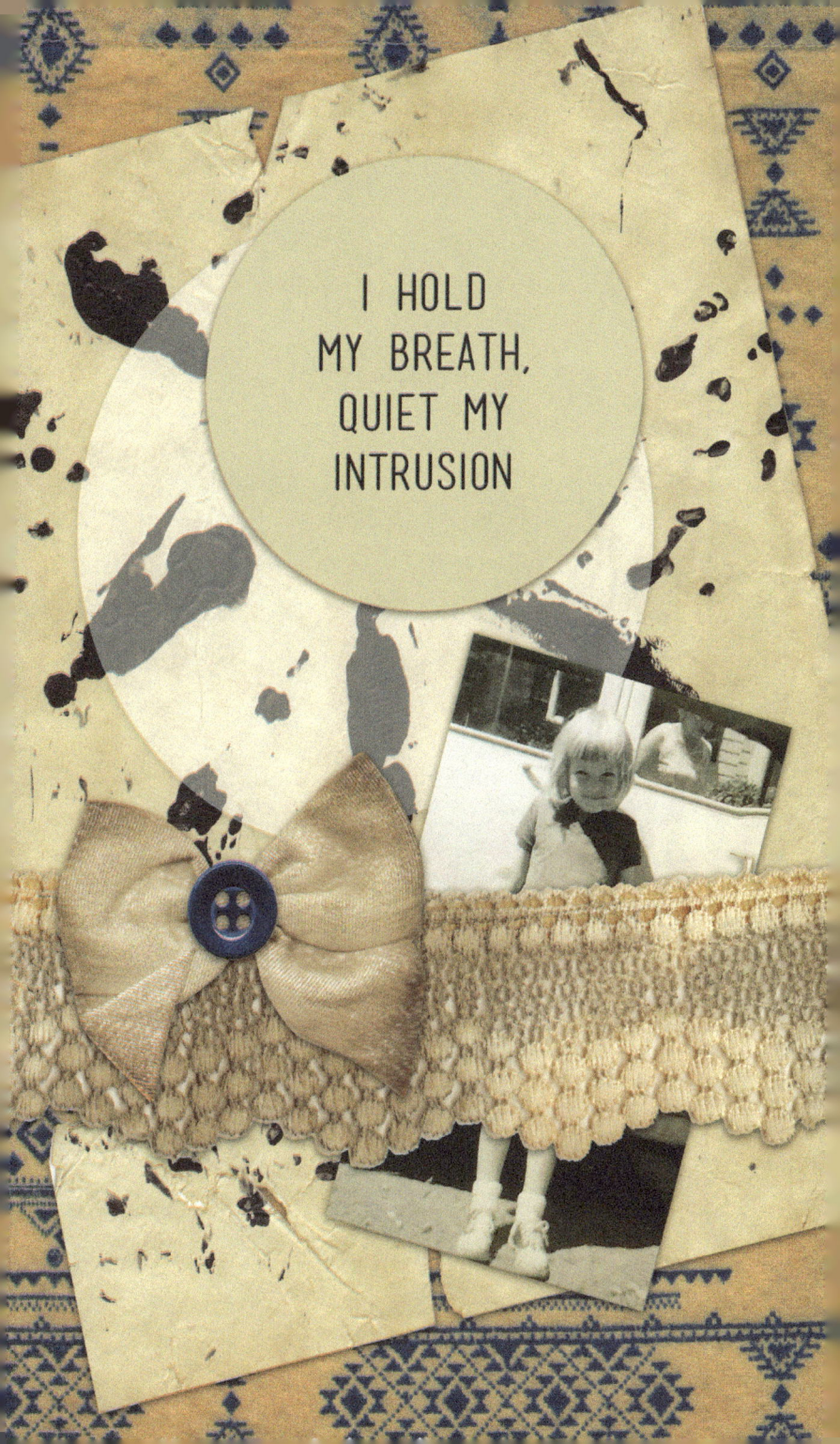

*For my mother and
her grandchildren,
Perry and Molly, who
bring beauty to my world.
Your vibrant spirits
continually inspire me
to be a better person.*

I love you madly!
Mom

House Key Necklace 9

TV and Mashed Potatoes 15

The God Bracelets 21

Fallen From a Nest 31

Stray Cats 37

Five Dresses 49

Regarding Animals 69

Waterways 77

Designing a Life 91

Shortest Marriage, Longest Love 105

Life Preservers 111

Raising Babies 115

Buddha and Bigfoot 125

I Didn't Learn to Play the Ukulele 133

Adult Dating 141

Missing What's Missing 149

Cloud Theory 155

A Rainbow of Gratitude 169

Becoming a Piece of Work 179

Accident Prone 185

Building Houses 191

© 2024 Cheryl Welch
WelchDesignPublishing.com

INTRODUCTION

My mother did not dress me, but if she had, my life would have become the basic beige that draped her long, short years in circumstances seemingly beyond her control. I love her for what she couldn't find and how the distance between us allowed me to explore the world through creative endeavors. I wish she'd lived long enough to see how her four children turned out. I think it would have made her happy.

    Having created a fantastic living patchwork of children, friends, and lovers, I stitch together these essays with love and care. I am grateful for memories of my children wrapped by friends whose kindness dressed them in beautiful mismatches conjured from their own children's overgrowing. It was wonderful to encounter the parents of a Chianti blouse paired with the most delicious Tuna Salad pants. Pure love from top to bottom in gracious disharmony!

    I remain secure in knowing that every color lives within another color, having once been primary until set free on a painter's palette and blended with a knife. This memoir speaks to the resilience found in challenges. I hope my readers find something to hold onto or embrace.

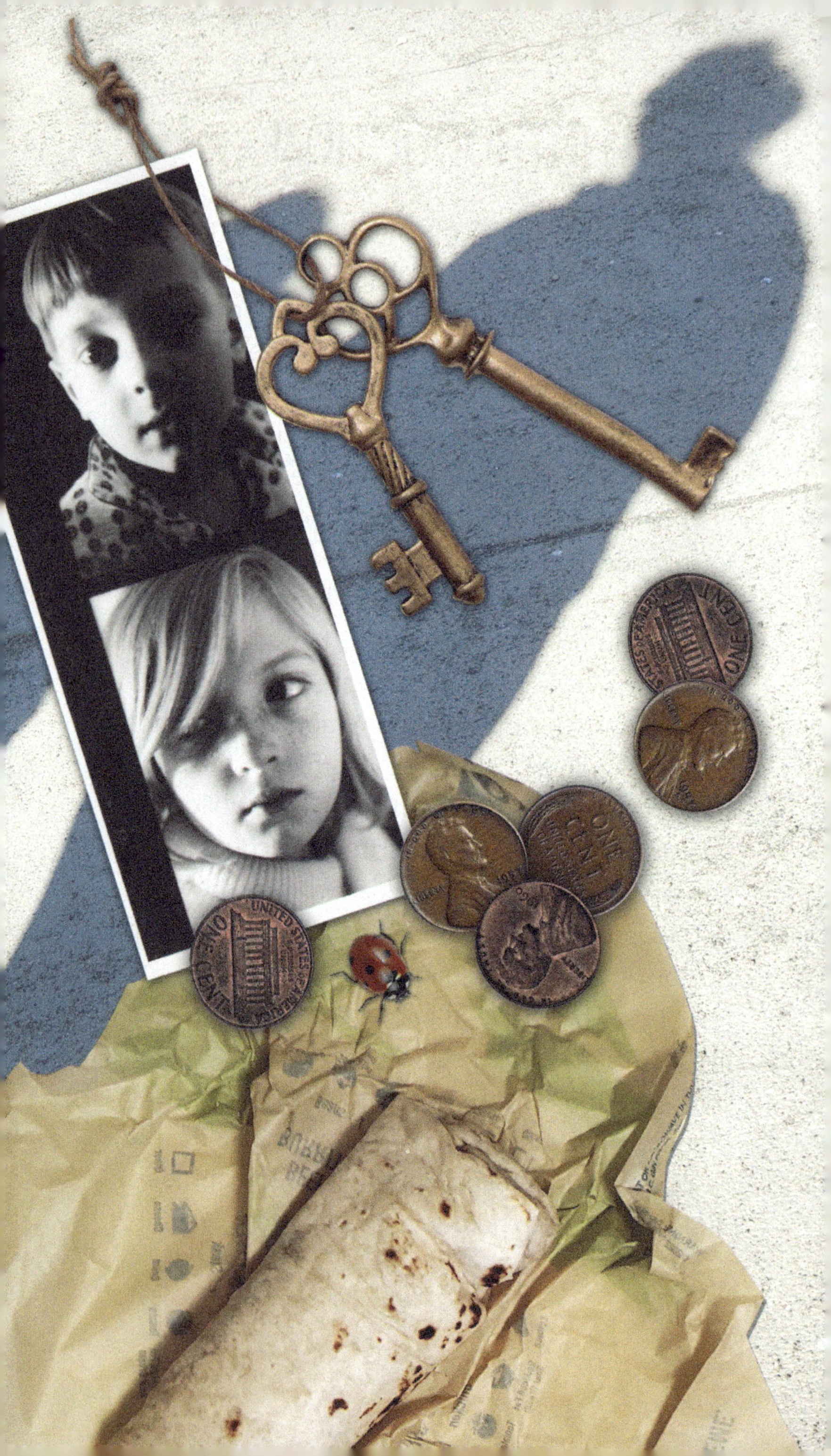
ONE CENT

HOUSE KEY NECKLACE

*let life hold you like a child on her way home
from the first day of school,
mistakenly wearing a necklace that is
the wrong shape for her face*

* * *

We all knew a kid or knew a kid who knew a kid. Yep, the one who attends school while wearing their house key around their neck. We were the pioneers of the Wild Midwest with parents at work, ponying up to our usual picnic table and straddling the bench alongside the other kids whose houses were empty at lunchtime. We were the spilled milk and weird smells of chaos untamed, reaching for hope in our brown paper bags.

It was the Day of Two Miracles. My little brother and I found our usual table. In our milk-money envelopes lay the first miracle, 6 cents instead of the usual 3 cents for milk. Good Lord, we'd been gifted chocolate milk today! My joy quickly changed to horror when the kid beside me knocked over my adorable, be-strawed carton. I followed, unable to move, the chocolate river that flowed to the edge of the table and water-falled onto the future history of my white skirt. Though only in the fourth grade, I assimilated the event as a guiding principle for much of my life. Temper joy with eventual and inevitable disappointment, but try not to cry over it.

We hurried our lunches in anticipation of any remaining time slated for "I will not hesitate to kill you" Dodgeball. We sipped chocolate milk while checking out the weaker children as initial targets.

After dutifully tidying up our tables, it was game on. I removed my glasses, knowing the expense of replacing them could ruin my family. And, even though hitting above the waist was forbidden, I was keenly aware that the super-pale boy across from me—the Elmer's Glue drinker—would not be averse to breaking rules. I stood resolute with my team, having had only moderate success removing the chocolate milk stain from my white skirt. "I am wearing a target," I whispered to myself.

The Lunch Lady released the newly inflated

nine-inch balls from their mesh bag and placed them on the centerline. The whistle blew. Joyous rage escaped our lungs. We were the left-behinds and social misfits delighting in student carnage while our single parents toiled at jobs they hated. We did our best to prove worthy, defend our latchkey status, and recognize respect in another child's silent nod of approval.

The boys were a hot mess of harm, aiming for the noggin when the Lunch Lady wasn't looking. The girls tended to work within the rules, discerning the elegance of a plan. My little brother, the smallest of us all, used his brand of practiced mayhem. His speed would be an asset. His low stature danced with surprise trajectory. His aim was true, landing balls as precisely as his attempted punch lines during lunch. Were those jokes ever funny? We were never sure but thought it best not to question such matters of the heart.

We were savages, lone wolves, returning to our afternoon lessons with tiny lungs still heaving. Victory was ours, whether we had pegged the skinny kid or fallen victim to the older boys. None of us cried.

Surprisingly, it was not all downhill from there. Being in half-day Kindergarten, my brother was waiting for me in the Nurse's Office so we could walk home together. En route, we scoured the Taco Bell parking lot for coins dropped from hands that were too full to attempt their recovery. On a good day, we'd find enough to purchase an 89-cent burrito. This was a good day. The resulting second miracle meant a burrito would come home with us. We were unstoppable.

I pulled the house key from around my neck, opened the shabby door of the shabby house, and locked it once we were inside. We had work and play to keep us busy inside those walls. We were never bored, but we were lonely.

We were a children's storybook silkscreened in two flat tints. We were silent on our pages, unable to fill them with one good friend to jump from the tree with and all the marvelous bugs we'd never seen.

It wasn't until I became a parent that I discovered the empty keyhole shape inside myself that had not been filled with cuddles and learning, answered questions and time out-of-doors, games, and stories. My parents were divorced, and both had to work to keep up with what little we had. I had an opportunity to do better with my two kids. What I could give them was also a gift to myself. I created, for them, all that I had missed. They came out strong, funny, creative, and kind. They remember how, for years, we'd make all the Christmas presents we would give. We were never bored, and we were never lonely.

Many years later, I would claim a third miracle, having received a necklace made by my daughter. Her Pre-Kindergarten class had made these beautiful gifts, and she was beaming when she handed the little wrapped package to me. It held a miniature likeness of her, traced from her school picture and strung on a beaded cord. It was just the right key to fill that empty keyhole shape in my heart. It lives among my treasured life. Full circle.

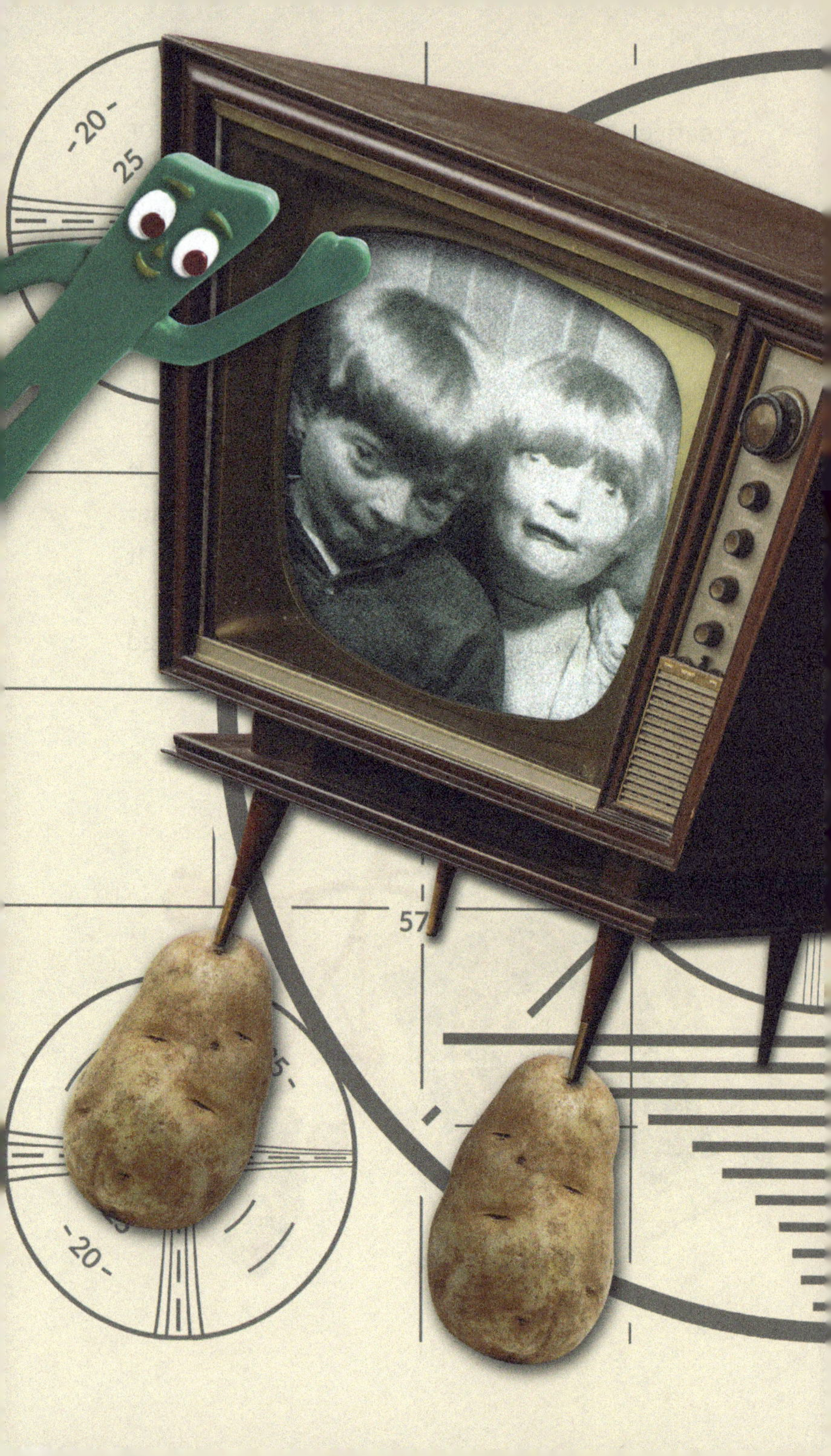
-20-
25
57
-20-

TV AND MASHED POTATOES

*if I were my own hero,
I'd courageously witness the telling of my story
with bullet points and graph line
upward trending*

* * *

Like many baby girls born in 1955, I was named Cheryl Ann. Watching the "Waterfront" TV series, our parents were mesmerized by the show's real star—a Tugboat named Cheryl Ann. It was not a common name for the time, and many moms and dads thought it was the most beautiful name they'd never heard. It ranked 19th in popularity that year and I encounter descendant tugboats everywhere that people "of a certain age" gather. The Cheryl Ann contingent is often found in the park, swinging their little boats, twice descended (tending their leaky bottoms), or catching their giggling life rafts at the bottom of a slide.

The colossal TV of my childhood would warmly welcome us home from school. My little brother, Jim, and I—safely locked inside our rented bungalow—would project ourselves onto the streets of Mayberry, enjoying the smell of Aunt Bee's famous apple pie. Perhaps Petticoat Junction would be our destination, as we quickly deemed Uncle Joe, its rightful hero for getting paid to "act" as if sleeping in every episode. That man sure knew how to shirk a chore!

We had our routine down. First, I checked the refrigerator door for dinner instructions. I was nine years old but knew my way around a kitchen. I learned how to scrub, pierce, and grease the potatoes before putting them in the oven at 350°. Each dinner, it seemed, included a baked or mashed potato, so I was a professional spud maker. Next, I would make the honey and mustard glaze, score and coat the top of the ham, and bake as noted ... good, good.

We had to clean our rooms, tidy the rest of the house, and set the table. Timing was everything, and I was a good motivator. We often ran while doing the housework, singing

"Stodola Pumpa," a Czech folk song from our youth, five times before returning to a central location, confirming the task completed, and then zooming off to fight for the vacuum cleaner over scooping the cat box. This day was not a laundry day ... good, good.

Having made short work of our work, we would have time for one more half-hour of TV before Mom arrived home. Dialing in the Three Stooges, we often made shrunken heads from clay or macaroni mosaic dinosaurs while we watched Moe double-slap his brothers and threaten to murder them. Whatever we crafted spent the rest of its artistic existence glued to a paper plate.

We made gifts to give or cards to send. We'd draw, paint, or sing into a cardboard toilet paper roll. It was a creative time, filling the emptiness with learning to care for someone younger, creating a schedule, and maintaining a home. These were good skills to have.

Our older brothers were not latched inside with us. The twins were Seventh Graders, and no one ever knew where their Seventh Graders were. Mike and Chuck would arrive home each evening when all the neighborhood parents stood outside their doors, hollering the names of their overdue adolescents. Whether my brothers were home or not did not keep us from eating my delicious dinner, smelling of roasted love, when Mom arrived home from work.

After dinner, it was Mom's turn to the TV. She was all in for The Lawrence Welk Show and for exclaiming how lovely the Lennon Sisters had grown. My pleas to stay up past bedtime to watch the Beatles on The Ed Sullivan Show one night were almost in vain until I tearfully howled that ALL of the other kids would be watching! She relented. It was the nicest thing I can remember her doing for me. Most of the time, I was pretty sure she didn't much care for me. She was tired. It wasn't her fault. She was disappointed in the hand she'd been dealt and didn't know how to draw for a second chance at winning. It wasn't my fault, either. I wanted her to love me, but it wasn't in our cards.

Other times, Mom would visit her neighbor friend after dinner or go for coffee with her boyfriend. I'd help Jim with his mimeographed homework sheets before heading to my room to review my growing collection of Beatles photos and listen to my transistor radio; I could almost touch the world outside my door, but it would be quite a while before I could join that world.

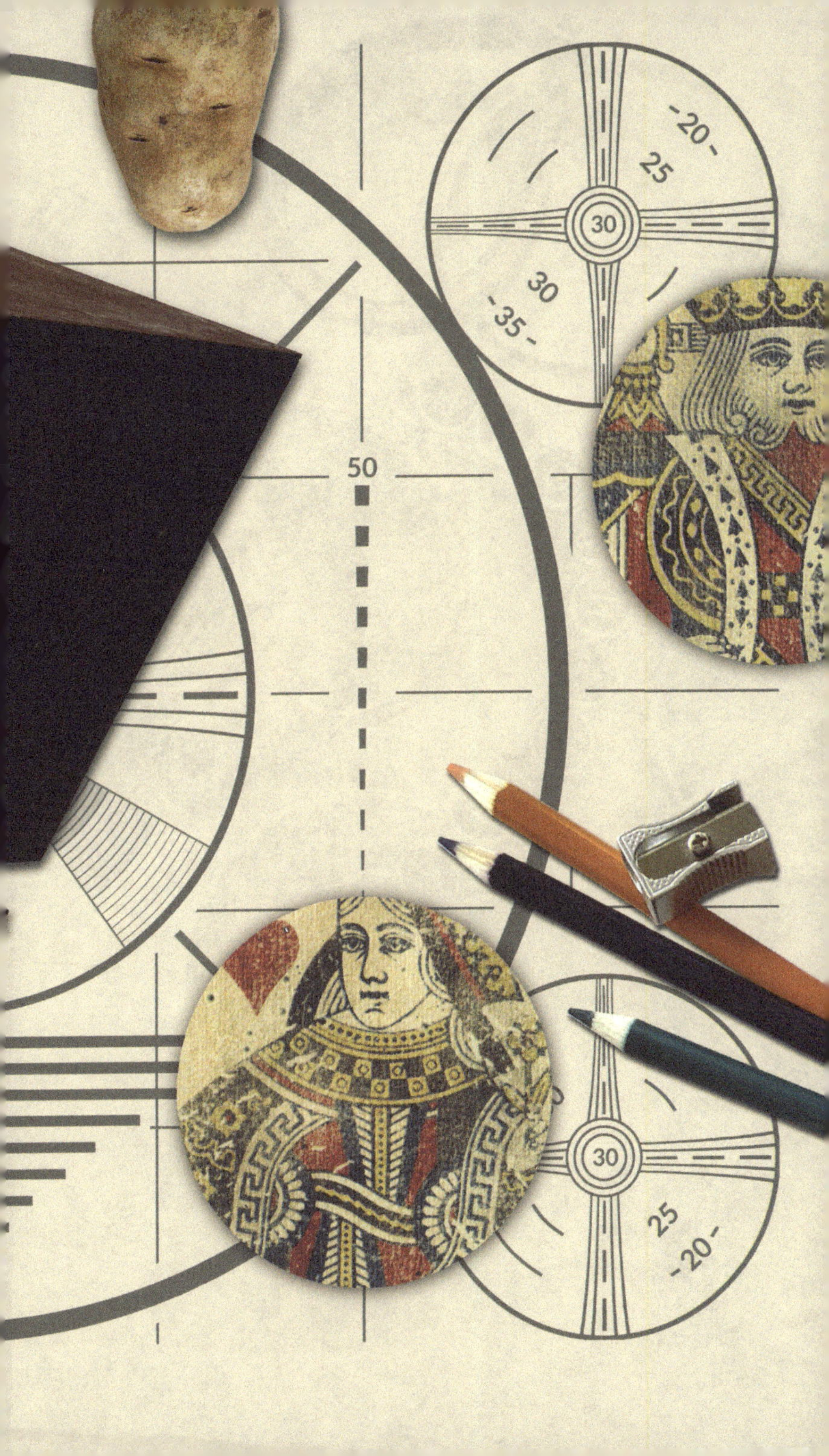
-20-
25
30
30
-35-
50
30
25
-20-

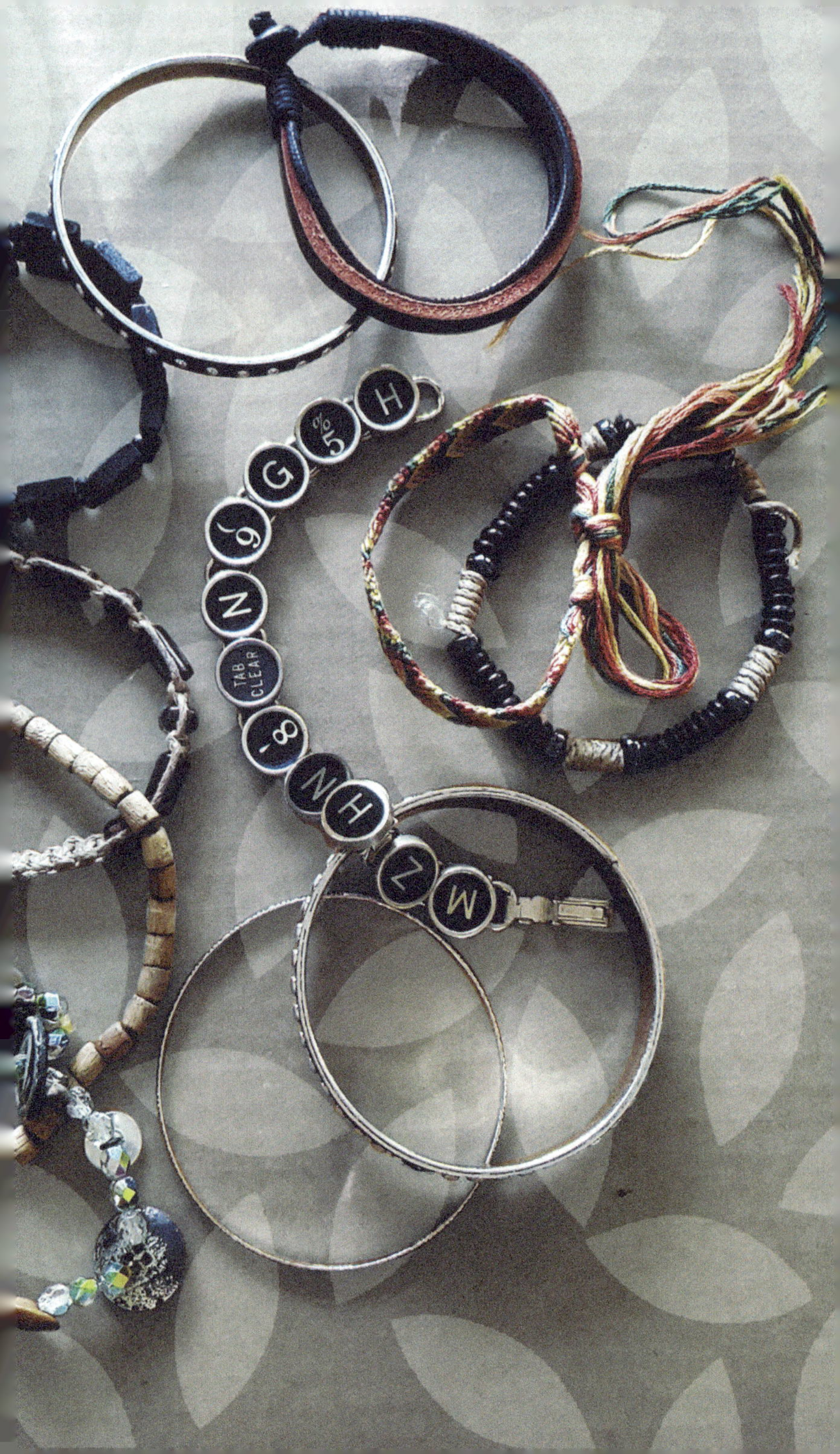
TAB CLEAR

GOD BRACELETS

our words flutter in bird wings
that beat the clothesline where we've hung
all language to dry in the hot sun

* * *

If your heart becomes too full of loneliness or happiness, so full of love that you mistake it for sadness, so topped up that you can no longer hold it in your own body, consider spilling a bit of it into someone else. Allow yourself to overflow. Let them share your pain, love, and words you discovered years after the Brimstone Day. They may not understand what you're saying but tell them anyway. Your heart will have space to beat after that, and theirs will be fuller for listening.

Give a bracelet you've made of your words to someone who may not deserve it because, in the end, you'll have more bracelets than you can wear in one lifetime while they may have empty arms. Make someone laugh so hard that they beg you to stop because they're exhausted. So pause briefly before reminding them that it's not how fast you mow; it's how well you mow fast!

* * *

In third grade, my classmate Susan found a bracelet on her way to school. She showed it around before placing it inside her desk as the bell rang. I sat behind Susan. I stared at that bracelet all day, thinking it was the most beautiful thing I'd ever seen. It was 2 inches wide with nonstop sparkling rhinestones strung on six elastic bands. A queen must have dropped it from her carriage, or a movie star tossed it to the street after breaking up with the leading man who had placed it on her delicate wrist. I started hatching a plan.

I stayed back while the others began filing out the door in a recess frenzy of loud. I grabbed that bracelet so fast that I didn't even know it had happened. Stashed in a sweater pocket, I constrained my recess activities to watching the other kids play tag, which I never did anyway.

This being a Brownie Troop day, I had a little extra time after school to create my cover story. Genius! I would tell my mother that we each received such a bracelet in Brownies—just because! I knew she would never check with the other mothers; she was a loner like me. She did, however, call my father.

After homework, I admired my bracelet, feeling its weight on my little arm. Dad arrived after an hour's train ride from the city. This was not a good sign. I was asked to join him in a room downstairs, after which the door was closed behind me. Dad said, "I need you to tell me where that bracelet came from."

I started with the Brownie Troop story, after which he replied, "Try again." For the next hour, I followed that with at least 100 lies, each becoming weaker than the one before. I had found it in the schoolyard and saved it from going down a drain after the big rains; a bird had dropped it from its beak while flying overhead. And then the biggest whopper, I'd received it from a friend—in actual friendship. At this point, it was clear that I would one day be a writer of fantastic stories. My father kept repeating, "Try again."

I was weakened, hungry, and running low on "believable" stories. "It was on top of Susan's desk, and I took it," I replied shamefully. I didn't know it was "shame" on that day, only that I thought my father could never love me again. Sensing the shift in my tone, Dad whispered, "Try again."

" It was inside Susan's desk, and I took it when no one was watching." I exhaled in exhausted surrender, awaiting the sentence I would receive.

. . .

"Now, we return it and apologize," Dad replied.

. . .

"Anything but that," I prayed. "

After what little dinner I could consume, I was "marched" over to Susan's house. Susan's mother answered the door, so my first confession was to her. Then Susan was summoned for some of the same. I handed Susan the bracelet, saying I was very sorry for stealing it.

Susan's family was Evangelical, and my punishment would be God. I would attend church with them on Sunday. That seemed fair, I thought ... until I got there.

Unaware, as was my father, that I had been

placed on the Sunday menu, here is what I recall before turning into a tortured mass of sobs.

> My eight little years trembled to the center aisle, prodded by old church hands as the preacher descended.
>
> •
>
> He did not smile as he shook his hands above my carved-short bangs.
>
> •
>
> Scowling parishioners witnessed their preacher fire and brimstone my pale frame's eminent journey to hell and damnation for taking that which did not belong to me.
>
> •
>
> For good measure, he also said that my father would be burning in hell for having left my mother. I suspect he'd received notes about our "terrible" family.

It wasn't enough that I was small and owned nothing of rhinestones; I'd never been taught God or church. No one cared that my socks had fallen down because they had belonged to my older brother. It was beside the point that I'd made a mistake … that I had apologized for it.

I was hysterical when Susan's family dropped me back at my house. They seemed pretty satisfied with my noticeable "saving." I thrashed on the couch while trying to tell my mother that my father was on fire. Dad arrived from the city, providing proof that he was still alive. I could finally rest and process all that had happened.

The Brimstone Day profoundly changed my life's trajectory.

1
I have, to my knowledge, never lied since that day.

It is painful to even think about lying. It hurts like a house full of empty. Instead, when asked, I try to temper my truths with as much kindness as possible.

2
I have never (again) taken anything that did not belong to me.

When my sixth-grade friend clipped a bracelet from Henderson's department store, I asked her to take it back and apologize. She didn't know about the deep well that emptied my insides since the first and last time that I stole an obviously "damned" bracelet. She probably thought God would forgive this bracelet and anything else she did.

The next day at school, I was pebbled with insults and some random debris kicked at my legs by the 6th-grade girl gang—the fabulous sixth graders, not my gang that only had one member, no matter how hard I tried to recruit.

3

I have not since entered a church except for weddings and funerals.

My high school boyfriend invited me to see a replica of Michelangelo's La Pietà when it was touring churches in our country. I got through the church doors but could not go down the aisle, gazing patiently from afar as my boyfriend bowed his head and crossed his signs.

My first wedding was in a Unitarian Church where pot seeds were found under the minister's chair when he left the room. This church, designed by Frank Lloyd Wright, immediately removed any possible damnation. My second wedding—the one that mattered—took place in our living room with the following reception at the club where we met. Friends, family, my new husband, Don, and his fellow musicians played all night long. My third wedding (yes, that seems like a lot) was held on a floating barge on the Hudson River where an antique sunken lightship, complete with barnacles, had been raised and moored. The barge shifted uneasily on the river, and our hairstyles had puffed beyond acceptable parameters as a hurricane breezed through.

* * *

Since the Brimstone Day, I have worn many bracelets, and have also received them as gifts—a homemade Cheerios bracelet from my child and one of braided embroidery thread to signify friendship. I've threaded beads among intricate macramé and espoused the proverbial pearls of wisdom. I wore a bracelet for several years until my green wrist surrendered, with the name of a Vietnam soldier and the date he was missing in action. These are my bracelets of redemption and hope. They are the higher power I carry to guard against the brimstone embers.

A bracelet is a never-ending circle with unconditional regularity and complete perfection. It is a promise that will not be broken, a lesson about moving forward without fear of an end as we continue to circle our loved ones who remain behind when we are gone. I know I will have lived a life that my children will be proud of. What happens after that will be a wonderful surprise.

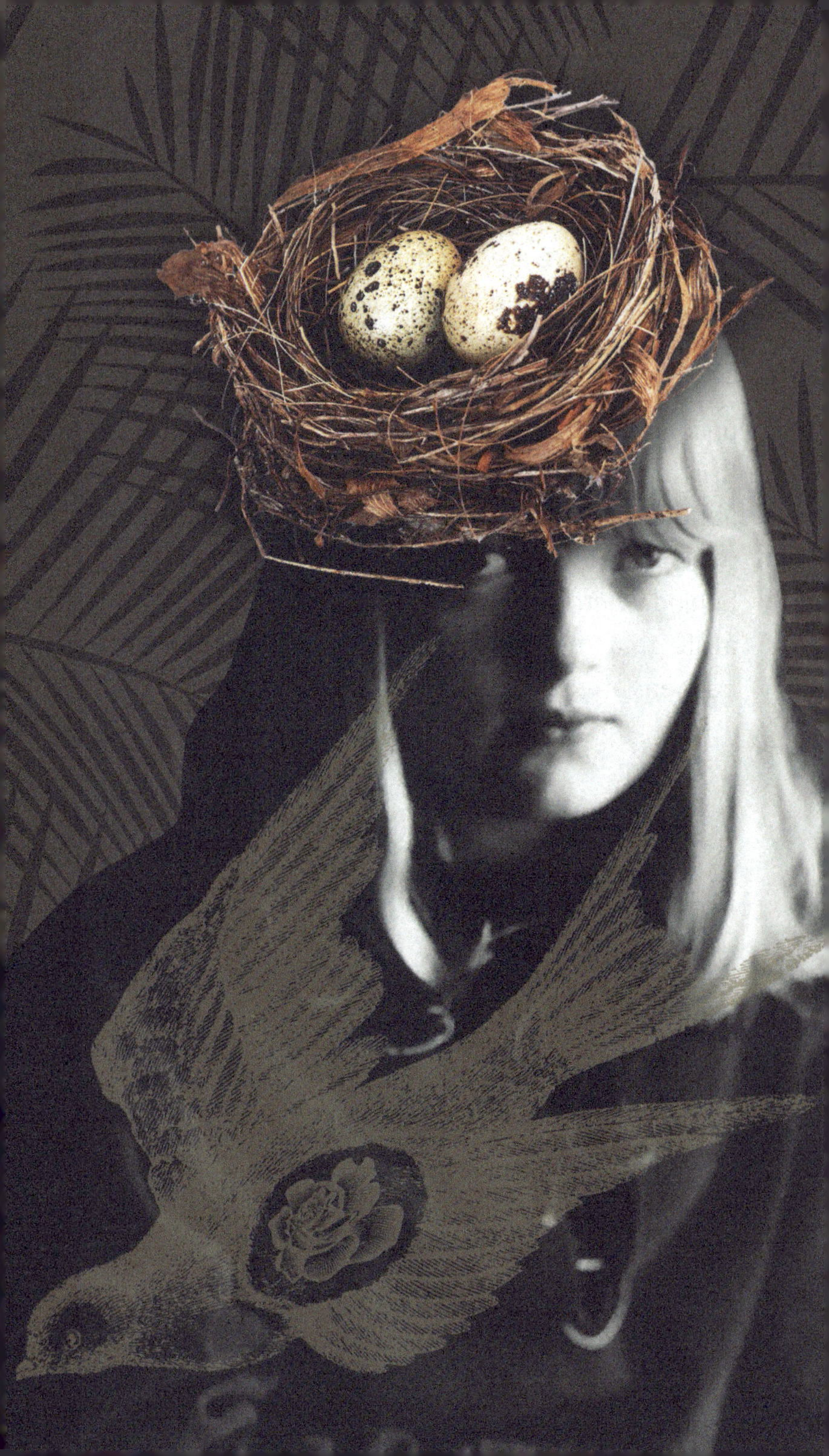

FALLEN FROM A NEST

climbing through blossoms
claiming a chair of branches, a fragile throne

* * *

This beautiful Sunday morning was clear and bright. The sun shadowed the base of trees and reflected off recently washed cars. The wind was more substantial than usual. It made music of the leaves in the cherry tree below which I sat reading.

I knew every inch of my yard in fallen twigs and overgrown grass strewn with gravel thrown wide by car wheels spun beneath a teenager's accelerator foot. Something laid out of place in this setting of regular irregularity.

It was an unexpected thing, this little bird. This tiny thing had fallen from the nest before being taught to fly. Mama bird, most likely off to seek food for her hatchlings, would return to find one missing if she could count, or spatially reason, the emptiness.

The little bird lay, not moving, near my size twelve-year-old shoes. It was dead. There was no need to modify or qualify the word; I knew it when I saw it. That little bird died, and I was the only one who would witness the loss of its future splendor, this never-flight of a left-behind. It felt deeply personal.

It was known in the neighborhood that, on the other side of my fence, lived a man who killed squirrels and birds. A hairy and horrid man whose lack of remorse and belt to hold up his pants would hang the murdered animals from the branches of his fruit tree as a warning to others who may try to feed among its leafy bounty. Even though I never looked over the fence to view the murder tree, I knew that large dead blackbirds and small gray squirrels dripped from its limbs. All the kids in the neighborhood were aware of the visual profanity on the other side of our fence and often lifted the smaller kids for a view over the chain-link edge of reason.

This helpless, blind, and naked baby bird, fallen and alone, stilled the breeze inside my body. Being hatched doesn't always guarantee flight,

I thought ... so I would stay with this little one until someone came home to tell me what happens next. I wanted to protect its remains from rabbits and cats that might attempt to carry it away. I watched the nest above me, examining it for signs of life. Mama bird had prepared a fine home, having labored in its building while preparing to lay her eggs and then turning them once laid to maintain their uniform temperature. She deserved to mourn the loss of her featherless babe, and I would sit in my church pew of tree-root until her return.

Being the weekend, my family members were off doing things that required going places. At some point, however, one of my older brothers returned. As I explained the situation, he seemed to be hatching a plan. "Do we bury it?" I asked. "No point in that," he replied, "a cat or some other animal will just dig it up." He went into the house, returning with a piece of cardboard to carefully scoop up the tiny bald thing I had forgotten to name. He stood briefly, cardboard stretcher flat out, holding some comical representation of former life. My brother assessed the likely scenarios before walking to our fence and flinging the little bird at the murder tree in our neighbor's yard.

I was speechless yet calm. In some way, it made sense that this bird's first flight through the air would end at the base of a tree adorned with its kindred. I was relieved of my stewardship, though greatly saddened.

***

Monday afternoon arrived after a distracted morning in my sixth-grade class. I usually looked forward to Monday afternoon, having been included in a special pullout group for honor students who met privately with our teacher to discuss challenging projects for the week. I could only talk about the little dead bird, sobbing at times as I recounted the sweet horrors of my Sunday morning while church-goers churched and recreationally minded folk recreated. When my teacher realized I was beyond consoling, she moved me to a small room near the principal's office so that I could regroup before returning to class. I didn't mind being alone in the fun-sized room. By this age, it seemed my natural state of being. I had fallen from my own nest at home and school, having barely begun to stretch my wings. In the quiet of this room, containing only a chair and desk (which I surmised was used for students in detention), I felt full of falling, my mind wandering around the edges of who might sit with me while I heal.

People frequently set off on a path and do not return to the nest. Some are spotted in flight and recorded by date, time, and directionality in family photos. I have flown high and far and have fallen in unexpected ways. My nest, now, is full of hatchings. My children have wide smiles and broad wings with which to stay aloft. We fly to each other as often as possible to nest in the soft leaves that cover the sticks and bits of feather that line our lives.

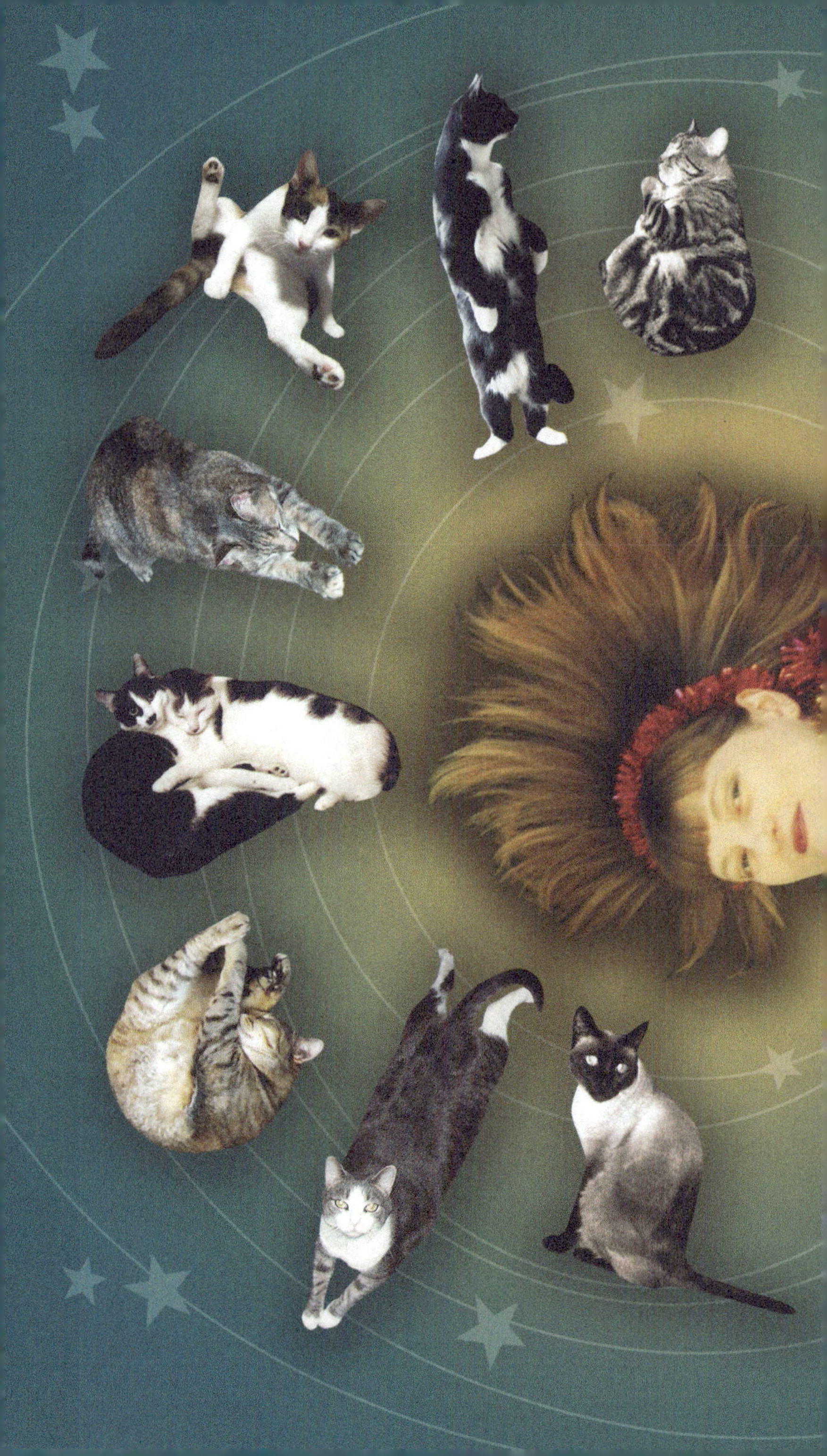

STRAY CATS

you were every window frame
waiting my return from the garden
to lick the salt from my busy summer hands

* * *

For most of my life, except for a few years at University, cats have encircled me. Over the years, there have been ten cats, including the mysteriously vanished Fritz, whose lessons live long after his disappearance.

In my memory, it was never clear where most of these cats came from. They'd been given to me by someone who couldn't provide their care or had been rescued from a shelter. They seemed to arrive just in time, knowing who they would be once grown into their names—though they were often surprising in temperament and digestion.

EACH OF OUR MANY LIVES ARE FOR LIVING

Being very young when the first of the squad arrived or when I first became conscious of her, my father tells me that she moved with us from Iowa to Illinois. She, being Tilly, was an elegant Siamese cat with the soul of a Hells Angel. Enjoying her cat lives as an indoor/outdoor cat, she spent a lot of time missing. She was with her gang of feline waifs and weirdos, returning for dinner and a warm child to sleep with.

We were concerned when she didn't come home one night or any of the many nights that followed. It was nearly a week when construction workers arrived at our door with something wrapped in a blanket. Neighbors had pointed them to our house after they heard Tilly's weak meow from inside a wall they'd earlier completed in a new home being built nearby. Emaciated but breathing, the vet was able to plump her back up with fluids, ready to begin her next adventure.

Over time, she'd used up most, but not all, of her nine lives. She'd come home dragging a leg after being hit by a car or with bald spots and bites from some larger animal. We'd rush her to the vet each time to have her trussed up or splinted.

Tilly was beautiful, inside and out, and so

thought the stray Tabby she brought home one day. He decided to stay. I called him Glenn Manning after the lead character in *The Amazing Colossal Man* movie. Quite fitting, I thought, as he was huge, but the rest of my family called him Joe. Tilly and Joe had wild adventures together, returning home needing a bath or bandage.

Joe came home one day with his jaw askew and bleeding. The vet surmised that some larger animal had bitten through his lower jaw. The doctor tied it to the upper jaw with some twine, and it healed eventually.

Despite her antics, Tilly lived for 20 years before succumbing to old age. Joe went off one day and did not return, no matter how many nights we'd spend calling for him. I hope he found another friend who, like Tilly, just wanted to see the world beyond our door. It had been a rough road for those two, and I have never again been party to any other than indoor cats.

KEEPING IS NOT THE SAME AS HAVING

I spent my first year at SIU (Southern Illinois University) in the dorm; however, after that year, I was allowed to move off campus, which was not typically allowed during the first two years, but I was vegetarian. They had no idea how to feed me. I was existing on salads and no parent wanted to pay for full-course, albeit Midwestern, meals when their child was only lettuce-worthy. I received permission from the Dean to move off-campus and was thrilled to locate a small basement apartment. I could feed myself on my food budget and was happy to leave dorm life behind. It made me itchy, and I was not a fitter-inner.

Returning home from school one evening, I found a little black kitten at my door. This male kitty was so tiny that I guessed he might have escaped from a new litter. I took him in, and he became Fritz the Cat. He seemed to hate everyone, letting only me come near him. He was feisty and always attempting a getaway. Fritz did curl up under my chin and let me bathe him. It was healing in a way I didn't know I needed. We cared for each other until he darted for the door one day and made it outside through my legs. I searched for him nightly and posted posters daily, knowing he was as wild as I once was. I hoped he and I would eventually grow to let people love us, even without a sense of belonging in any one place.

UNLIKELY PAIRS CAN BECOME TWO OF SOME KIND

Various felines entered my orbit as I continued to revolve around the sun. After graduating college, I moved into a studio apartment on the northwest side of Chicago. I found work, and a proper gas giant (trust me on this) named Cecil found me. A pretty calico, this cat was round, dense, and ringed in gentleness and sobriety. This no-nonsense cat soon earned the moniker "venerable old sir," ever ready for an iced rum or brandy, neat, at the end of a meal. He could be found seated in a chair, human-like, with a paw on his knee. He was a truth seeker, divining his quiet wisdom from considered watchfulness. Cecil was a loner, but the addition of Milton to our jam would surprise even the man himself, as he became a loving big brother cat.

Milton, a tiny tuxedo, wearing a tinier tuxedo, was very young when we received him from a neighbor down the block. He took to Cecil like a kitten to a mother, and Cecil, though male, was generous enough to pretend to nurse him. Milton and Cecil became the best of friends. They were Laurel and Hardy, bacon and eggs, Saturn and Pluto (or Dwarf Planet if you prefer).

Milton was wild, always running, fetching, and using Cecil as a jungle gym. Cecil remained ever the epitome of civility. This lovely bonding of opposites was delightful. I watched Cecil parent, growing beyond his cool exterior to fill my heart with warmth. For his part, Milton proved that being wild and somewhat unlovable is just the right prescription for someone who is quiet and needs to love someone else.

Cecil and Milton moved with me three times across Chicago, then to New Jersey, into a second marriage, and through the birth of my son. It wasn't long after Cecil's passing that Milton began losing his life in inches. He slowed and spent more time with his humans. I like to think Cecil and Milton enjoy a nightcap together, in their reclining chairs among the clouds.

A PERFECT VAULT CAN END IN NOT STICKING THE LANDING

After the birth of my second child and the passing of my husband, the little ones and I would soon visit a shelter to retrieve our newest family member. Perry was the first to fall in love with an older cat as others ogled the kittens. As we would soon name her, Phoebe sniffed my fingers from inside her too-small shelter digs. She and

I locked eyes, understanding that this family, minus one, needed her.

A bit of a nursemaid, Phoebe followed me everywhere, ensuring I was okay. She kept me warm by sleeping against my side, letting me know I was not alone. Phoebe would help to teach my children how to be caring and loving. A patient cat, she would succumb to Molly's efforts to feed her pretend food, read to her, or dance with her dangling from Molly's young arms.

Phoebe taught me how to be alone and my children how to be not alone, and we all felt loved for it. She would, years later, move forward with my children and myself after I met and married my third husband. We all moved into his house, and his cat, Pia, joined our revolution. It took a while for Phoebe and Pia to tolerate each other. They were not keen on sharing this new family.

Molly, four years old at the time, was afraid of Pia, who would sometimes nip at her ankles. I was summoned nightly to remove Pia from the top of the stairs as she glared at Molly's ascent to bed. As with many people I've encountered who find change quite difficult to overcome, most animals, including the two-legged variety, can be gentled—but sometimes they can't, and that's where we found ourselves at the end of that marriage. Phoebe became very ill and passed as our combined family began to unravel. Pia was left without feline companionship, and Abbey arrived to save us all.

ODD COUPLES

Arriving home from our local shelter with a young Calico female, my husband and I introduced Pia to her new partner. Abbey, as we named her, would sit on the edge of my desk or my lap while I worked, as Pia slept in a cat bed near us on the floor. They never found friendship with one another, but they did learn to coexist for a year until Pia departed this realm.

Abbey felt Pia's absence and shadowed my steps to the point of me tripping over her when I made a move. I knew her mothering instincts would be better served with a kitten, so a young tuxedo named Maggie joined us. Those two cats became inseparable. Abbey was a born nurturer, and Maggie was apparently a meerkat, standing upright whenever there was a sound she needed to hear more clearly. They were always cuddling, or reaching to place a paw on the other wherever they rested. Had I been able, as a child, to nap like that with my mom, I can't imagine how different my life might have been.

As Perry had already moved away, and Molly was living with her boyfriend, it became time for our marriage to end. Abbey, Maggie, and I moved to a studio apartment across town. For the first time in many years, I was alone with two cats as I had been when I was young. The kids were close enough to visit, but life had stalled for me, and I needed a big shake-up. It was time to leave New Jersey. Molly would join me, planning to attend school in California. Perry would stay in New Jersey to attend his budding duel careers as a teacher and musician.

I considered taking Abbey and Maggie to California, but it would have been hard on them to travel for seven or more hours in the noisy cargo bay of the airplane. I feared for their health and decided to return them to my ex-husband's care. Abbey later passed after a brief illness at a reasonable old age. Maggie still lives there today with a second cat named Dottie. They have made attempts to bond as we all had in that house.

THE LONG WALK HOME

Settled in my San Jose studio apartment, I attended a pet re-homing event at a local pet store. There was a gated area where the cats walked freely. I took a chair in the corner and waited for one of the cats to choose me. An adult Tabby approached and jumped into my lap. We went home together, and she became my Sophie. We will grow old together. She has been diagnosed with early-onset kidney disease, and requires daily blood pressure medicine. As my last cat, it is fitting that she is the most loving of the cats I've lived with. I, too, have reached a point where love matters above all else. I do my best to live in that space.

Sophie is a bright star, burning with pure light, following me room-to-room and climbing on my lap or shoulder whenever I stop moving—sometimes hugging my neck with both arms. She is, however, very respectful during the night, sleeping in her bed atop my bed and staying there until I wake. She waits for me to get out of bed before her, and then we walk to the kitchen, where I make coffee while she stares at her bowl until something delicious appears.

Oddly, Sophie is the first cat of all my cats that doesn't make a sound. She occasionally squeaks if stepped on, making the tiniest sound one can imagine. Our synchronous living is a powerful reminder of what I seek in my human relationships. I am no longer interested in arguing or rude behavior. We're all walking our paths for a short time. Perhaps we'll meet a kindred spirit to walk with for a while. That's what Sophie is teaching me to hold in high regard.

***

My feline sensei have taught me the importance of living fully, inviting me to recognize the joy in play and the reverence in holding someone close while napping in the sun on a breezy day. It has been an honor to care for these little beasts, to call them family, to hold their paws and say, "Thank you," as they pass. They've shared their company and their crazy, listened to us fight low and sing high. Each has been a fount of healing and forgiveness, for if we can provide for their comfort and safety and unconditionally love the hissers, biters, and clingers, then surely we must have value in the world.

5

FIVE DRESSES

*I will devour your shadow in any shape
it arrives, knowing it will never
be less than everything*

* * *

Five dresses live large in my memory, each having traveled through time from humble origin to esteemed companion. They speak of challenge, chagrin, commitment, callowness, and being cherished. Each dress, in its way, reminds me how we build best when we build together or that the price tag for love may be self-doubt. One resulted in receiving my Activist and Drivers permits in the same year. Another remembers that not all mirrors reflect equitably, so we must be our own heroes. One teaches that if we love as fully as possible, possibilities grow like children constantly needing new clothes.

❶ THREE-ARMHOLE DRESS

I credit my introduction to sewing to Girl Scouts of the USA. As a junior scout in the fourth grade, our troop worked on a sewing badge. We each purchased the same pattern, McCalls Wrap-A-Rounder Dress, and fabric of our choice in the appropriate yardage. Reading pattern instructions is a lesson in patience. We calculated our yardage and had the sales clerk cut the proper length of bias tape. We matched our thread colors and cheerfully arrived at our next meeting with materials in hand. During this meeting, we pinned the mysterious transparent pattern pages to our fabric, carefully assuring its position in harmony with the fabric weave. We tucked our little pieces of brilliance into the Girl Scout designated cubby in our school's all-purpose room before gathering in a circle to sing *Taps* to close the meeting.

During our next meeting, leaders placed giant scissors on each table, warning that these "shears" were sharper than the stubby cutters we used in class. Like surgeons, we cut methodically through the pinned pattern pieces and the successive layers of folded fabric. We carefully removed the pins, secreting them away in pincushions. Each girl would follow instructions at home, using their own sewing machines to complete the three-armhole dress.

No one questioned whether each home had a sewing machine. It was the early 1960s, and seemingly by osmosis, every mother had a sewing machine or had brought their mother's machine to their married homes. There would always be a need to stitch a gift, an article of clothing, or reconnect a seam in their child's well-worn pants. Moms helped their scouts to guide the fabric and mind the high-speed needle. Most of us would complete our dresses by the next meeting. These frocks of magic wrapped around one's body one-and-a-half times, with a third armhole securing the dress without need for buttons or zippers.

A miracle of dedication and achievement was completed after the final pattern step, trimming the edges with folded bias tape. The final stage to procure the coveted sewing patch was to press our creations. I starched, steamed, and tortured that dress to within an inch of its existence. It was the flattest, sharpest-edged dress among the troop. Mrs. Johnson reviewed our dresses and announced that we would wear our three-armhole dresses to the badge presentation at our next meeting—hot damn.

Being a member of the Girl Scouts taught me many things. Of course, I learned new skills, but it felt like family. I was one of Mrs. Johnson's 10 children, whom she loved equally and praised earnestly. In my adult years, I felt inspired to create such a family. Living in Hoboken, New Jersey, at the time, I contacted the Girl Scouts of the USA and volunteered to be a Girl Scout Leader. In an effort to reach under-served areas, I was to start a troop in an apartment building on the west side of town. The families who lived in the multi-story building included parents who worked during the day, and the girls would sometimes be alone after school. After securing a ground floor room for us, I set a day and time and put up posters.

Our first couple of meetings brought in a few girls, and we discussed how we'd like to spend our time together. The numbers grew, sometimes including younger brothers the girls were in charge of until their parents arrived home. Another life loop closed for me, having received this opportunity to love these kids latch-keyed in their homes as I had been as a child. I could care for them in the way that we all deserved.

I realized this Girl Scout troop would have to break rules to succeed. A meeting at the Council office and I had permission to include all ages and a few boys among the girls. I asked for donated sashes, as purchasing uniforms would burden their families, and a flexible track to earning badges. The Council assigned a Co-Leader to our troop, and we met to plan meetings, parties, games, and dances. We, most often, just had fun. Occasionally, we passed out badges to the girls who followed our custom path to achieving them. Seeing the older girls assisting the younger ones and helping us leaders as needed was gratifying. We were a family. I hope that they remember their time in scouting as fondly as I remember mine. I hope they felt proud of themselves and each other.

❷ A BOWL OF CHERRIES

There is a sweet spot between graduating from grammar school and entering junior high. After leaving sixth grade, one has a summer to grow the distance between child and teenager. I imagined that my classmates would page through *Teen Magazine* to study the fashion trends and read about how we should feel and think at this age. Some needed to know the appropriate age to begin kissing, how to dress thin, or discover if they have what it takes to be a stewardess. I pictured them reading together while gathered in the popular girl's bedroom, discussing if tall girls should date short boys and how swearing could ruin your reputation.

I spent my summer looking after my little brother, suggesting that my older brother "bite me," and feeling ill-prepared for what lay ahead. September approached, and I was ready to be in class again. I was eager to meet my new favorite teachers and make friends. When the weekend before school began arrived, it was time to shop for a new dress. I had already made a lavender-flowered skirt with a matching headscarf and still had a few dresses that fit, so one new dress would suffice. My mother took me to

Montgomery Ward ... to the Junior Department, where I chose the most beautiful dress I'd ever seen. It was empire wasted with a high collar and long sleeves. The fabric—white background covered in a field of delicious cherries—begged to follow me home.

I was excited to attend junior high. It was a quick walk down the block from my house and required changing classes per subject matter. It was all so exciting. I wore the cheery-cherry dress on the first day of school and about three days every week after that. It was the best thing in my world that year, and I wore that dress to smithereens. I wore it so often that some kids started making fun of me. I was surprised when I chose to care instead of telling them to "bite me," as my brother advised. I felt small inside that big dress, and even though it swirled around me like a tent, it was still not big enough to cover my shame. I can't remember who mocked me or what was said; it felt like I had committed a crime contrary to the 12-year-old rulebook. I subjected myself to a jury of one (me), the harshest judge I've ever encountered. I decided not to wear it for as long as possible.

If carefully accessorized and plotted on a calendar, I would have enough outfits not to repeat so often. I would wait to wear it on the occasional Friday while kids were focused on weekend plans.

I kept my head down and did the work during my first year in junior high. I got good grades, with Math and English being my favorite classes. I grew fond of the teachers in those classes, found a foothold in my schedule, and began searching for my gaggle of girls. My superpowers included seeing the invisible kids. Awkward hats, oversized glasses, and too many freckles would find my lack of charisma irresistible, and we began to gather at the same lunch table. To my surprise and delight, my glorious gang of four girls all loved Star Trek. We soon assumed the identity of our favorite characters. I was Bones McCoy. Our Kirk was a magnificent leader who kept us on task. Our Mr. Spock had a big brain full of facts and was not afraid to use them, and Scotty would keep us laughing with her terrible Scottish brogue. None of us wanted to be a female character. We chose to be the stars deemed best for pretending we were not weird.

I soon suggested we make Phasers out of toilet paper rolls. So an afternoon of paper maché and paint resulted in arriving at school the following week with them hidden in our purses. I liken this to a first-ever virtual reality game with an emphasis on reality. We would discreetly evaporate designated Klingons with our Phasers. We would sometimes shoot each other—set on "stun," of course—to keep it lively. We built several-day stories around the teachers and students whose celestial bodies we would navigate. Mr. Spock became my best friend and never mentioned that I was wearing the cherry dress too often.

We were deliriously happy when graduation arrived. Due to the week's laundry oversight, I crossed the stage as "the girl in the cherry dress." I cried before promenading to receive my diploma dressed as a bowl of cherries, which I fruitfully hoped to grow out of by eighth grade.

❸ PANTS-LESS

The dress that impacted my life and my future as an activist wasn't a dress. It was a pair of pants. Around 1971, rumblings began among the girls in our high school and neighboring school districts. Wherever girls gathered, they could be heard saying, "We have to organize a walkout." It had been a dress code policy until I was 16 years old that girls should be required to wear dresses or skirts. Not only are Midwestern winters among the harshest, but that's a lot of time to keep the boys from looking up your skirt when seated or climbing stairways. A brief dalliance was attempted by school board members, allowing "culottes skirts" as a possible alternative. It was better than a dress but only made us thirsty for more.

We girls took matters into our own hands, setting a day for the walkout that would include girls from all area school districts. We walked out during the 5th period with signs, and heard a few brief speeches before going home. It was poetry; it was fighting for a cause. It was only a short time before the school board voted to relax the dress code, which would now include pantsuits and dress slacks for girls. We won.

I learned the value of working for just causes. It wasn't long before I found myself among the Students for a Democratic Society (SDS) near the end of their reign, with a locker full of forbidden handouts, free speech stickers, and pins. The school Principal searched lockers constantly, but our group had stashed the goods in my locker because my National Honor Society credentials and unbearably mousy exterior removed me from suspicion. We did our work to create fairness in our schools, and I continued, as an adult, to advocate for women's rights and the substantial power in each vote in every election.

Before my classes' twenty-year high school Reunion, we were invited to submit a memory to include in the Reunion program. Mine read, "Sorry, Principal Rider, the SDS contraband was in my locker the whole time."

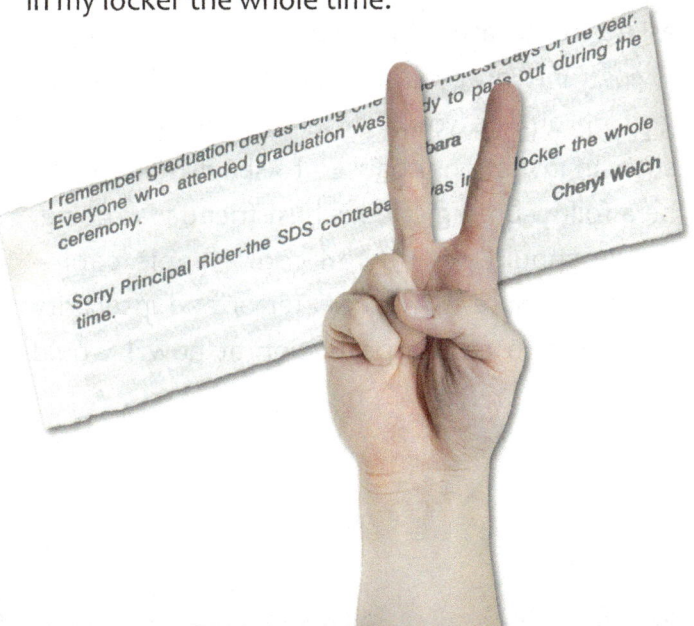

❹ PROM SUIT

I spent many perplexing years in high school. My Star Trek friends grew up and spun into their separate universes, but I hadn't seen the point of growing up yet. Fortunately, I had other things to entertain myself while reliably making the honor roll.

I loved my art class and learned how to use paint and other materials that I gleefully added to my Create-a-Latch-Key-Kid toolbox. English was my second favorite class because we wrote stories and poems that quickly led to my joining the high school's literary and poetry magazines. It was the first time that I'd had an inkling of the person that I would like to be. Just as the stars had begun to align, a cosmic shift attempted to blow my mind. The boyfriend of my waking dreams asked me to attend our junior prom. He looked lovingly into my eyes and said, "You don't want to go to prom, do you?" Unsure of how to answer such an invitation, I paused to see if there might be a follow-up. He said his best friend was going, so we should go. I acted cool—hippie cool—and said, "Sure, why not." Terror and insecurity combined to cause speculation at how I would pull this off.

I was sure it would be cost-effective to make my prom dress, so I headed to Henderson's department store and found a pattern for a floor-length halter dress. I played it safe with an inexpensive white fabric, as I wasn't sure what I was supposed to look like and had yet to find out what my date would be wearing. As prom neared, I discovered that my boyfriend would wear a pale blue tuxedo jacket with black pants, so I trimmed the bottom edge of my dress with some floral tape with blue flowers.

I eavesdropped on chatter in the high school cafeteria and tried to discern what girls were doing for prom. There would be manicures and hair and makeup appointments. I discovered that most girls would wear wraps as the temperature might be a little cool, and it was a fancy way to dress up a dress. I was running out of time to make anything like that, so I went to Montgomery Ward and bought a twenty-dollar white blazer. That's right; it had officially become a prom suit.

The results were horrifying. I didn't trim my hair, so it just wasn't good. My face was okay; I didn't wear makeup and wasn't concerned about that. My father traveled out from the city to photograph me in my prom suit, as I did my best not to stand like Lurch from *The Addams Family*.

My boyfriend arrived, and a second mugshot of us together was taken. My boyfriend said, "I like your natural look,"—uh-oh.

In the early 70s, big hair was on the rise. The prom showcased a dazzling display of hairdos raised like skyscrapers. Some girls had hairstyles piled loose and high with a cascade of ringlets to frame their faces. I spent the evening trying not to look like a lump of coal among these diamonds, these beautifully gowned girls whose organza dresses flowed around their feet on the dance floor. Their cover-ups of gauzy or fringed shawls draped photo-shoot style over arms or on the backs of chairs. They wore wrist corsages and held tiny purses. Most had shaded eyes and pinked lips. It was evident that I had attempted prom on my own without the benefit of teen magazines to offer guidance.

Looking at that picture now, I think, where in the world was her mother? I only knew where Mom wasn't. So I was in my prom suit, a wrong-side-of-the-track kid attending a right-side-of-the-track event. The Prom Suit lives its memory bittersweet in its innocence and dreadful in its legend. I recognize that kid, grew up with her, and wish that I could have been the lucky one to be her mother.

Prom Suit

A LOOK THAT INSPIRES CONFIDENCE

HALTER BACK

SEW NATURAL

72¢

LEGEND 1717
SIZE NOT AVERAGE
1972: A SEW NATURAL PATTERN

LEGEND | BE A TRAIL BLAZER

1717 SIZE NOT AVERAGE

SPORTY BLAZER DOUBLES AS EVENING WEAR

HAIR ALERT: FLAT IS WHERE IT'S AT

DELICATE FLORAL TRIM

⑤ WEDDING BELLE

There are times when everything you know rests comfortably in your days. Fingers lace perfectly in hands that stroll an avenue. Ideas are respected, and smiles come quickly. It was this way with me and Don Brody. It was a feeling that moving forward was the only way we could move, and we only wanted to move that way together.

I asked him to marry me, and he replied, "Yes, but I don't know when." I could wait; I was pro-level at waiting for things and people. I had waited for this one person forever and could wait forever more.

My forever wait turned out to be one year. We planned our wedding to coincide with the anniversary of our first date. I was excited to have another dress to think about. I decided that I would make a skirt and I would buy the top. I had no plan except to begin, which is always the best plan. I had a brief love affair with a bolt of fabric before sweeping in from its shelf and taking several yards of it home. It had a background of black lace and was appliquéd with purple and white satin ribbon flowers. It came together effortlessly, as if mice and bluebirds had sewn it while I slept.

Likewise, a first rifle through the fancy rack at Saks Fifth Avenue produced a top that pulled me into its sleeves as if a forgotten friend. This white satin, off-the-shoulder peplum top had a white rose gathered from the fabric and sewn at its bodice. In our one year together, Don had shared a million white roses with me, actual roses and figurative flowers that arrived in words or deeds, sometimes in his song lyrics. I bought the top. I considered it very expensive and had never spent that much on anything. It was 500 dollars, twice as much as we spent on both wedding rings combined, but it made me feel like a billion bucks.

I opted for black half-boots, and the completed ensemble couldn't have been a more beautiful representation of what I felt inside. I loved every minute of being in that dress and feeling its promise. We married in our living room, where, one day, I would read books to my son and watch him dance to his dad's music, as only babies can. It would be the room where we plan to buy a house and consider adding another child.

Arriving later that evening at the club where Don and I had met, we greeted guests at a wedding reception that included musicians

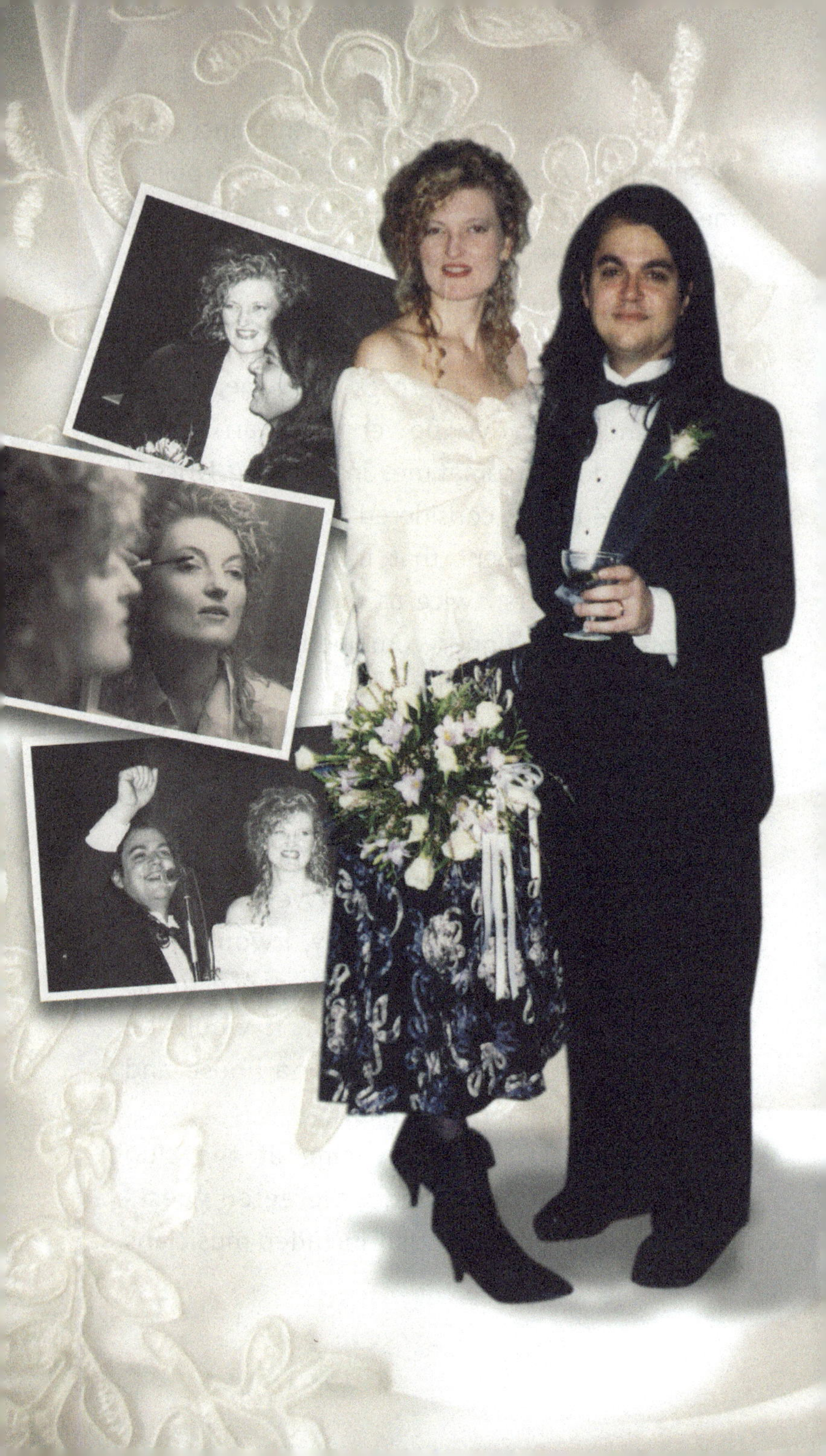

who played, and laughter and hugs were as bountiful as the beautiful buffet and flowing tap. My homemade wedding dress twirled as I danced through everything I could ever have dreamed possible in this one night, this perfect dress, and this big life. I felt a part of something larger than myself; it was a family of my own making, and I would forever make it a place of acceptance and delight.

Don and I met on November 17th and married on November 17th of the following year. We thought it would somehow create good fortune. In the uncertain certainty of all things "universe," this number kept appearing in our paths. Our son, Perry, was born on January 17th, and our daughter, Molly, on July 17th. I was grateful that Don's sudden passing did not fall on a seventeenth day or year.

The kids and I continue to find random 17s everywhere we go. We take pictures of them and send them to each other, feeling that Don Brody wants us to see that he's looking after us or that we must be attentive to the road ahead. Perry, Molly, and I plan to get matching "17" tattoos the next time we are together, a tangible reminder to live our lives full of funny and indomitable courage.

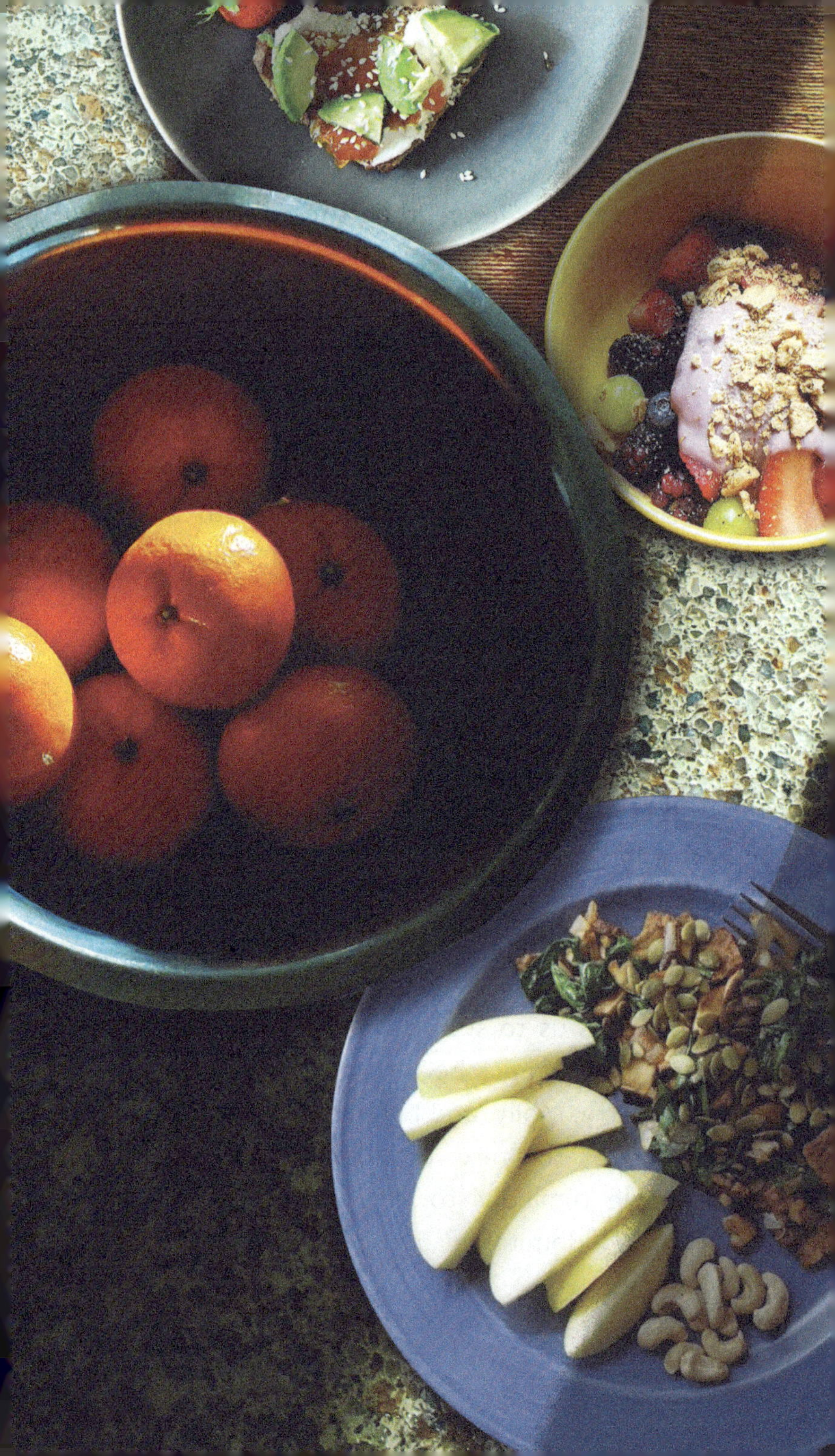

REGARDING ANIMALS

not targeted but still precise
caustic and heavy I carry your pieces,
emotional residue in my arms and legs

***

Despite my young career as a budding Julia Child, glazing ham and pounding meatloaf to perfection, I have not eaten meat, fish, or poultry since I was 14. Over the past twenty years, I have further eliminated dairy and eggs from my diet, becoming a total vegan chick. All told I have been vegetarian or vegan for over 55 years.

If you are young and decide this may be right for you, don't tell your older brothers. In my case, the twins, three years my senior, began taunting me with talking strips of steak when I was only ten years old. They chased me around the table with hamburgers whose lifted buns would "moo" loudly, and don't think for a minute that they would miss an opportunity to walk a pair of chicken legs up to my plate while making a clucking sound. Fortunately, when Mike and Chuck started high school, they had far better things to do than pick on a little sister.

***

As a youngster, whenever I looked pale, had a cough, or felt tired, a nearby adult would usually say, "It's because you don't eat meat." It wasn't. A tour through the family scrapbook is all one would need to conclude that I was born the color of milk and continued to boast that shade of skin until the end of my latchkey days.

Once out and about, however, the sun was unkind to my Swedish and Irish skin, blistering it to a fiery sleepless red that made clear I would require the most enormous hat a small girl could wear without it being weird. It was still weird.

The lack of sunshine during my childhood seems to have served my skin well—my current color is more oat milk than cow's milk, which seems appropriate. I am quite healthy, having only a little Arthritis in my hands and feet, but that seems natural and manageable. So I want to talk about the animals.

***

I was so in love with animals of all kinds, watching how they move and think, loving purely in their animal ways. I have always felt closer to their kind than most humans I encountered, and wanted to save as many of them as I could. I asked my mother if I could stop eating meat, and she said, "When you're old enough to cook for just yourself, you can do that." So I continued doing my job as head chef, preparing the animals served but skipping them myself. It's fortunate that I loved the potatoes and canned green beans ever-present in Midwestern homes.

By the time I turned fourteen, the family dinner had flown by the wayside. My brothers never being home and my high school activities taking precedence. I began cooking my meals, following a lifestyle I knew was best for me. At this young age, I was unaware of the abuse animals suffered from the beginning of their short lives to becoming a bit of something on someone's plate. In the years since my decision, I have learned of the terrible conditions in which they were kept and hoped that more people would come to respect the rights of all animals to live free.

I believe that "animals are here WITH us, not

FOR us," as Earthling Ed (Ed Winters), a noted vegan educator, public speaker, and activist, has been heard to say. Still, over my half-century of following this animal-free diet, I've never lived with anyone who shared my dietary preference, including all husbands and my children. I have also never had a friend with whom to walk this path. This has seemed strange to me, but everyone must make their own choice in such matters. Speaking about it, here, is an exception to my "whatever works for you" rule that I've employed my entire solitary-solidarity life.

I stumbled upon Earthling Ed several years back and love how he approaches people to speak about veganism. He is caring and thoughtful and keeps asking them logical questions about consuming animals. Seeing them think about it for the first time is impressive. Ed doesn't force his views; he only offers logical reasons why animal injustice may suggest a move toward veganism. His efforts, including some beautiful TED Talks, may have changed some minds.

***

After moving to California, I was a member of the Sweet Farm Animal Sanctuary in foggy Half Moon Bay for years. Sweet Farm supported farm animals rescued or given up when they were no longer productive in the farmed animal industry. On the farm, these mistreated animals—including cows, pigs, sheep, chickens, goats, and a llama—spend the rest of their lives free from abuse, roaming together in large pastures. Member Days were so much fun, learning about the farm, and hanging out with these fantastic beasts. The cows, clearly in love with their caregivers, would also allow us mere mortals to caress their heads, as they half-closed their eyes in gratitude.

As the California coast experienced drought and wildfires in the summer of 2020, the farm experienced thick smoke, causing them to evacuate the farm for two weeks. They decided their Half Moon Bay location was no longer sustainable. A year later, plans were in place to move Sweet Farm across the country to upstate New York. They have relocated to an area where water flows through land and pours itself from the sky. I hope they are thriving and growing.

***

It wasn't easy to be a vegetarian when I was young. However, I hadn't yet given up dairy, so there was always something egg-like or cheesy easy to prepare. There weren't many vegetarian or vegan products in the stores during this time. Today's grocers are chock full of vegan offerings, and the list of products continues to grow. I love the bold "Vegan" labels on brands that also include non-vegan choices. There are, too, whole grocery stores primarily committed to this healthier lifestyle. I'm so pleased for the animals, and grateful to the companies that make saving some of them a little more accessible.

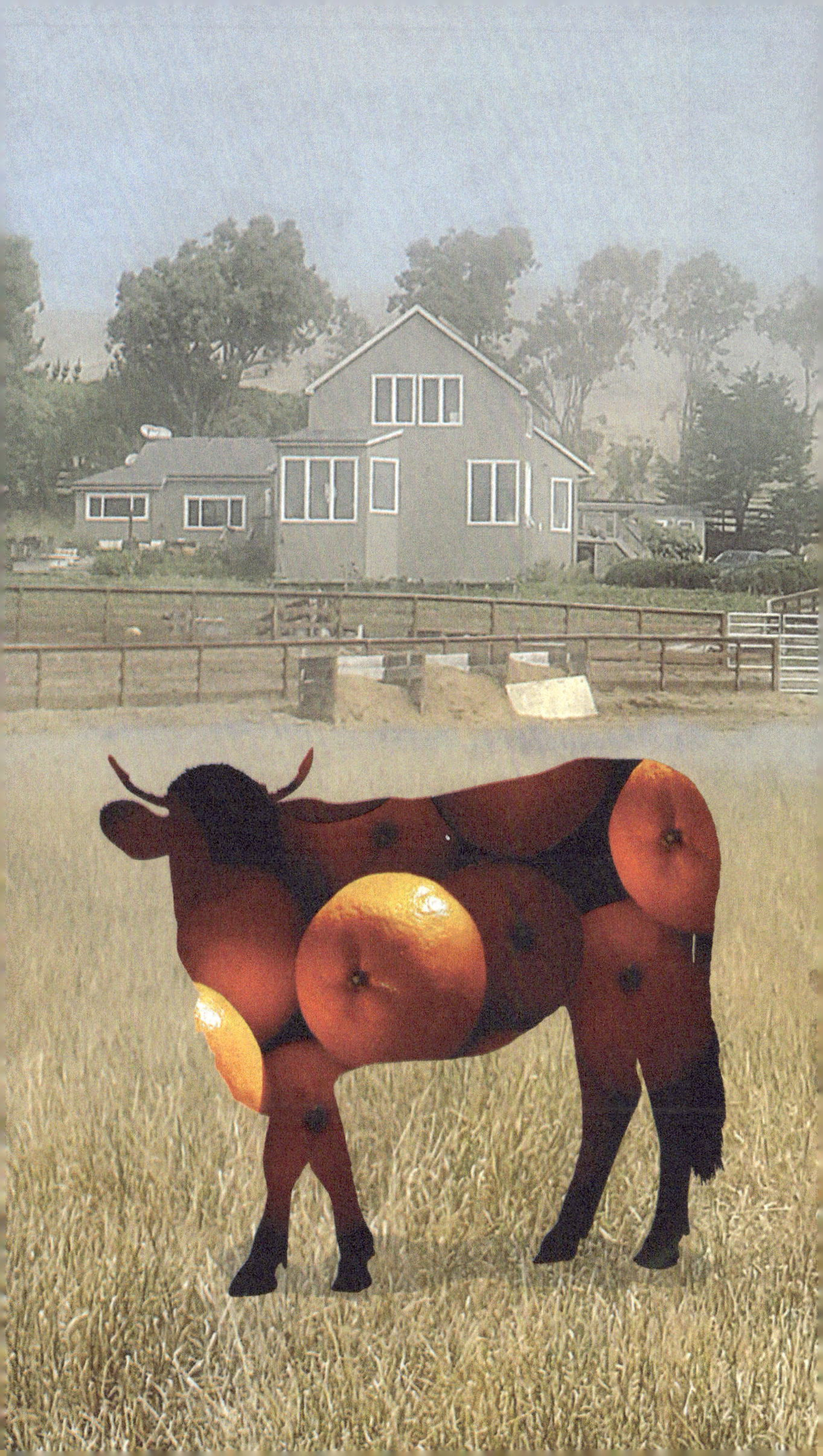

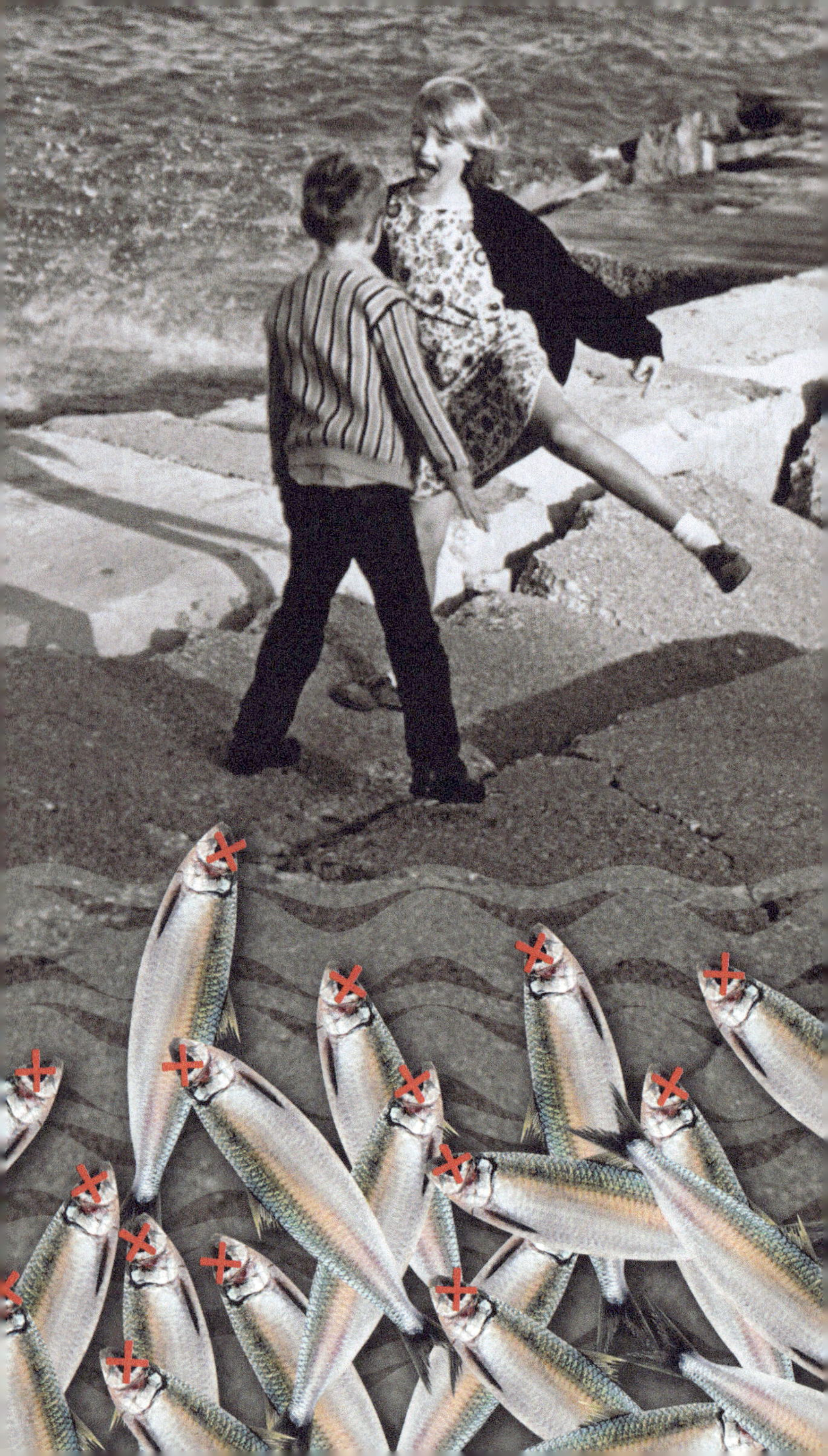

WATERWAYS

waves fill my digging, run quickly back
to the water's edge
this too, is a way of living in my lack of language

* * *

My life seems connected by a series of waterways. This notion is ironic since I can't swim due to an unfortunate occurrence when I was young. I was at the town pool, ten years old, watching my friend jump from the diving board into a small rectangle of deep water where heads bobbed before quickly scattering outward to make room for the next diver. The lifeguard was chatting up a bikini as my friend stepped forward and bowed her head. As I stood at the pool's edge, a young boy ran at me from behind. I heard his awful little feet slapping the wet concrete before planting both of his hands into my small back. Winded and unable to swim, I fell hard into 13 feet deep water, holding onto what breath was left in my lungs, thinking that I would hit the bottom of the pool and launch myself up to the surface.

Time, being fluid, felt much longer than the possible 40 seconds I was in the water. I could not find the bottom of that pool, so I began flailing in the darkness of closed eyes and scattered thoughts. My skinny arms reached for anything I could touch, hoping another swimmer who would know I was struggling would pull me to the top. I found nothing but an ache in my chest and hope swirling the drain.

I struggled in what felt like a swimming motion until I reached the surface and reached for the pool's edge. Gasping with relief, I had not perished in that airless mass from which others popped up laughing and splashing. I edged around the pool until I found a ladder and lifted myself out of the pit in my stomach. I felt sure that the boy, whoever he was, would be laughing and jostling his pals at the sight of my near wasting. I felt ashamed at my lack of swim skills that everyone else possessed. I told no one. Water had won. I never again was in water that I could not rise above while standing.

At age thirty, I decided I should know how

to save myself should I ever again be surprised by a water event. I went to the YMCA and took the "minnow" level class with the other little ones. I did not put my head under the pool's surface but learned to tread water, float on my back, and breaststroke my way forward. I passed, proudly receiving my Minnow Certificate along with the other children.

***

The most significant of the waterways I've traversed is Lake Michigan. In fifth grade, my little brother and I would take the train from Lombard to Chicago to spend the weekend with my father. For 36 hours of most weeks, I was just a regular kid under the care of a parent who, though I did not know him well then, seemed to weave art and music into a beautiful life. Furthermore, he wanted to share it with his weekend kids.

My father worked and lived in Chicago, so a trip to his office meant visiting Lake Michigan, whose beach began just beyond the doors to the Playboy Building, where Dad was Creative Director for Playboy Clubs and Hotels.

One magical year, we joined other Playboy employee families at a Christmas party at Hugh

Hefner's Mansion on Chicago's "Gold Coast." The Jackson Pollock in the ballroom seemed the size of a suburban lawn and held a universe within its four corners. In an uncharacteristic feat of bravery, I slid down a fireman's pole to the basement swimming pool. From the lounge area at the bottom of the pole (that first step off the edge was terrifying), one could be served drinks while looking into the pool's interior through a plate glass wall. Young women swam like dolphins, rarely breaking the water's surface for air, or perhaps they were snitching oxygen from scenic plants within the pool. I could scarcely believe my good fortune to have witnessed such a spectacle—from the safety of a dark bar and a cushioned seat.

When I was in sixth grade, my father moved to an apartment that was mere steps to the lake. As always, Lake Michigan was vast and inspiring. It also positively reeked of dead Alewife. Let's talk Alewife for a wee bit. The poor creatures died in heaps at our feet for several summers during the early 1960s. Initially from the Atlantic Ocean, these small fish found their way into the freshwater of the Great Lakes via the Welland Canal near Niagara Falls. Temperature change and lack of zooplankton needed for survival tossed their little carcasses ashore in great numbers. The Alewife were piled so high that bulldozers were employed to remove them. It was freakish to see and smell so much carnage while sitting atop our beach-boulder thrones; the sand and water stretched beyond our imaginations. The lake's endlessness marked my becoming the person I would primarily be for the rest of my life, grounded but forever looking toward the horizon.

We continued our weekend visits, though growing school activities sometimes required our regrets. I was Captain of the Archery Team, and that equipment wouldn't carry itself onto the bus. I had joined the staff of my high school literary magazine and had my sights set on a young man as well. During this time, Dad lived near Lincoln Park and was part of Chicago's folk music scene. Our weekends often included time spent at The Earl of Old Town, home to many great musicians coming to the fore in the mid-to-late 1970's. We were treated to the likes of John Prine or Bonnie Koloc. The infamous "Lincoln Park Pirates" singer, Steve Goodman, lived in my Dad's apartment building. For his part, Dad was a regular at the Earl's open mic, and I was an irregular at guitar lessons on the second floor above the bar. We were hippies. You could just feel it. And Lincoln Park goers could see it as we flew a kite we'd made from a Bob Dylan poster removed from a wall.

Those weekends with my father were filled with creativity. They were singing into a cassette recorder. They taught us to harmonize and to play chess. We collected rocks, shells, people, and experiences. We learned the importance of activism when knocking on doors for McGovern. Those 1,872 hours annually would more than double my life otherwise lived in the latch of keys. Those years wrapped my shoulders like a warm blanket through a cold night. I chose my career path during these years, having watched it add so much to my father's life. After high school, I studied what was then called Commercial Art at Southern Illinois University, launching a 45-year career in Graphic Design.

***

After leaving college, I returned to Chicago to find work as a Graphic Designer. I took the elevated train from my near-north apartment to The Loop, an area of track circling the south end of the river. The Chicago River swam through Chicago's business district and glowed neon green on St. Patrick's Day. This fluorescent mapping of city locations was both shocking and delightful.

I worked at Studios in this downtown area. It was a remarkable time of growth and opportunity. I was fortunate to work at a studio that designed packaging for Kenner Toys and was responsible for the Play-Doh and Alien package designs. I learned to art direct a photo shoot and mock-up packages for the Toy Fair in New York and attended the event on one occasion. Let's discuss New York. Boy, Howdy!

During this time, I met my Starter Husband, an artist, and we married a couple of years later. We eventually moved to the East Coast to seek our fortune as artists. Landing in Hoboken, New Jersey, we staked our claim on the cheap side of the Hudson River, and I found a job on the other side of that river in the American Express art department. There were two ways to cross the river: under or over. I chose the ferry, which became the two bright spots in my commuter days. Over time, I explored every inch of that ferry's upper and lower decks and became familiar with its regular passengers while constantly checking under my seat to ensure that its cubby contained a life jacket.

***

The Atlantic Ocean was about an hour from where I lived on my new coast. My starter marriage ended, and through a miraculous series of fortunate events, I met and fell in love with the man who would become the father of our children. We would spend time at the ocean, watching the world widen around our children's astonishment. The sound of voices and crashing waves filled the hollow sound of a hot day.

I would usually stay with Perry near the water's edge, ever mindful of the undertow and rarely letting go of his hand. Don would blanket himself and Molly under an umbrella, as she was under two years old. Our soaked and salted skin made our growing family feel itchy with excitement as we collected rocks, shells, and memories.

Seeing Don with his children at the ocean would remind me of a phrase he was known to say. We'd been talking about how to teach our kids to safely enjoy the water when he said, "No problem, I'm a fish." As a child with polio, he would be free from the difficulty and pain of movement while swimming in a pool. Hearing this would fill my heart with gratitude for my health and for meeting this man who would teach me a thing or two about living, cementing ever after the meaning of keeping my head above water.

***

Years after Don passed away, I was married for a third time atop a floating barge on the Hudson River ... during a hurricane. Everyone's hair was a fright. Our original plan was to hold the wedding inside Light Ship Frying Pan, a vessel built in 1921 to join the fleet of American floating lighthouses. The Frying Pan sunk in 1986 and was raised in 1987 to join the other dozen surviving American Light Ships. Taking our vows inside this barnacle-ensconced piece of history was the kind of unique experience we'd hoped would be memorable. Our wedding was unforgettable—and then some—but not in any of the ways expected. The ship had taken on water, so the staff set us up on a barge next door to the boat. Guests could still tour the Light Ship if they didn't mind getting wet.

The barge was well covered, and the staff protected the band. Still, the impending hurricane made for a rocking dance floor as occasional wind gusts would temporarily blow down the tarps and mist the dancers. It was one of those things that you just had to roll with. Folks were soon wearing pirate tattoos found buried in their individual treasure chest party favors amid gold-covered chocolate "coins." Surprisingly, more than one person proclaimed this debacle "the best damn wedding ever!"

Our marriage would last eleven years before circumstances dictated that another move was in order, first across town for a couple of years and then across the country. California would be home while my daughter attended school in San Jose.

***

I continued to work remotely from my dandy little studio apartment in California. My new ocean was about 40 minutes away and dazzling at sunset, smelling of seaweed and recently vacated shells. My nearby piece of the Pacific Ocean was also home to the International Dog Surfing Competition and "the world's most beautiful" (as it is known) Taco Bell, built right on the beach.

I was able to work remotely until the Coronavirus pandemic forced my retirement. My New York clients could not hold industry events in person and did not need graphic design services. Finding work in California proved futile as the world had temporarily stopped moving forward. I'd been thrown upon this new shore and circumstance, now having to plan a different life. It was an easy choice. I would be a writer. I took every online writing class I could afford and began publishing and illustrating my books. I did make time to drive to my beach, masked and safely distanced, for the occasionally much-needed sanity break.

***

My new ocean is fresh water; its beaches are either sparkling white sand or covered in boulders that shelter sea and land creatures. Giant waves roll with bits of broken shells and seaweed, gifting them briefly to the shore before reclaiming them in a fierce undertow.

The sunsets defy description, swallowing my awe and any words I may reach for. The sky burns with more stripes of color than imaginable before the sun drops quickly below the horizon, leaving a contemplative afterglow. This place feels like belonging—not only to those who gather nightly at the shore to witness the day's end but also, ultimately, to myself.

I had not read the cliff notes about California rain. There's a lot of it during the winter. For us optimistic folk, it becomes difficult to imagine a rainbow at the end of it when it never seems to end. Walls of water slice through trees and telephone poles, keeping the days from being seen altogether. It's difficult not to feel one's spirit dampen when thinning skin feels every drop of every downpour. The wind is often gusty and rattles the windows in their frames, just enough to remind me that life is precarious at best. Trees bow in the wind outside my window as a cat sleeps soundly on my legs and coffee brews. There are plenty of warm, dry places to gather for music and dancing, and I've made friends that I feel I've known forever. If I move from this shore, I have tucked so much of this place into my soul that it will no doubt travel with me.

***

I've grown deeper for having bridged these bodies of water. Lessons found in their bold splashing and gentle flow have buoyed my safe passage from childhood to adulthood. I have earned my invisible water wings, which keep my head above water and keep me moving forward, albeit often against the current.

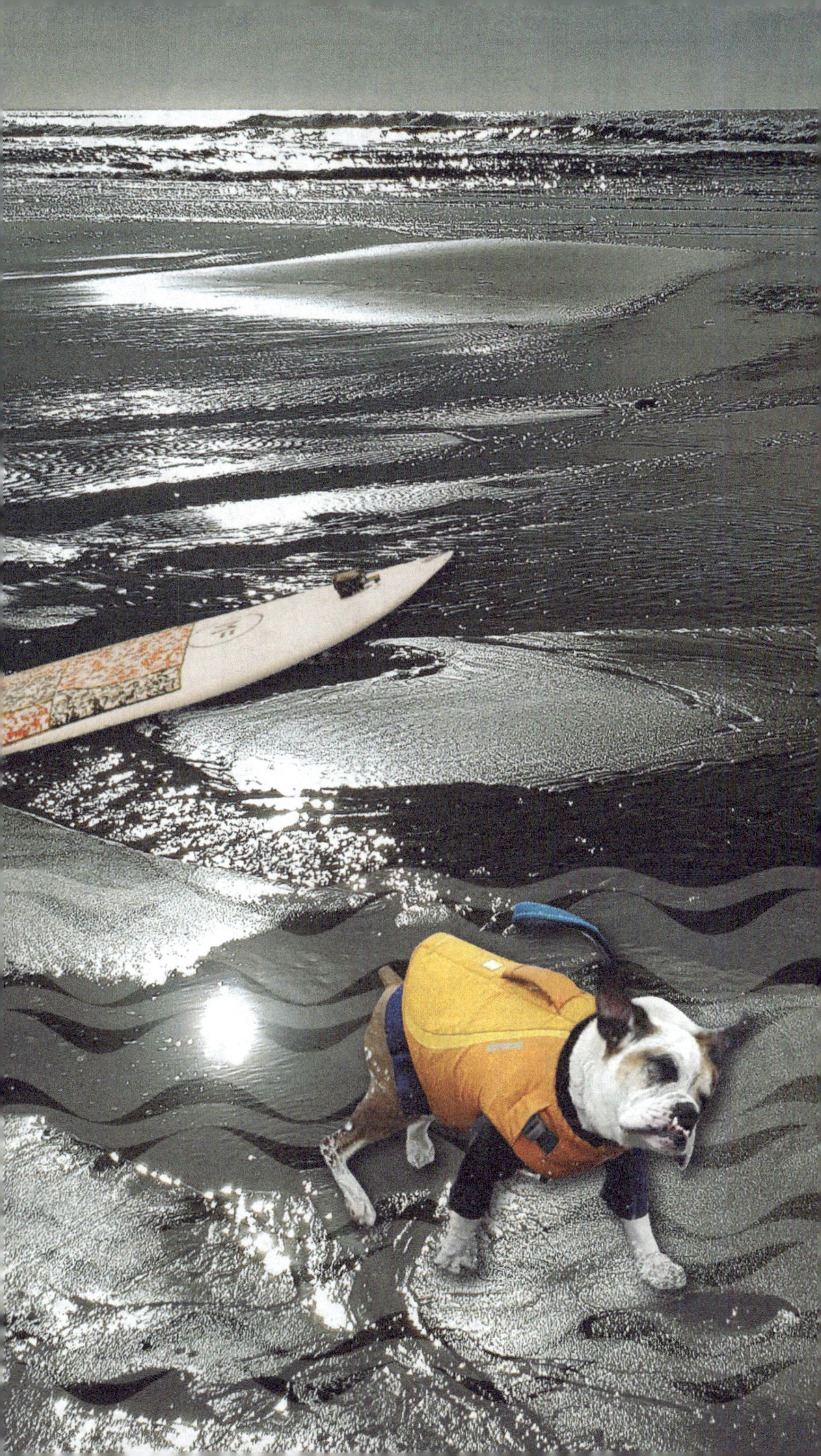

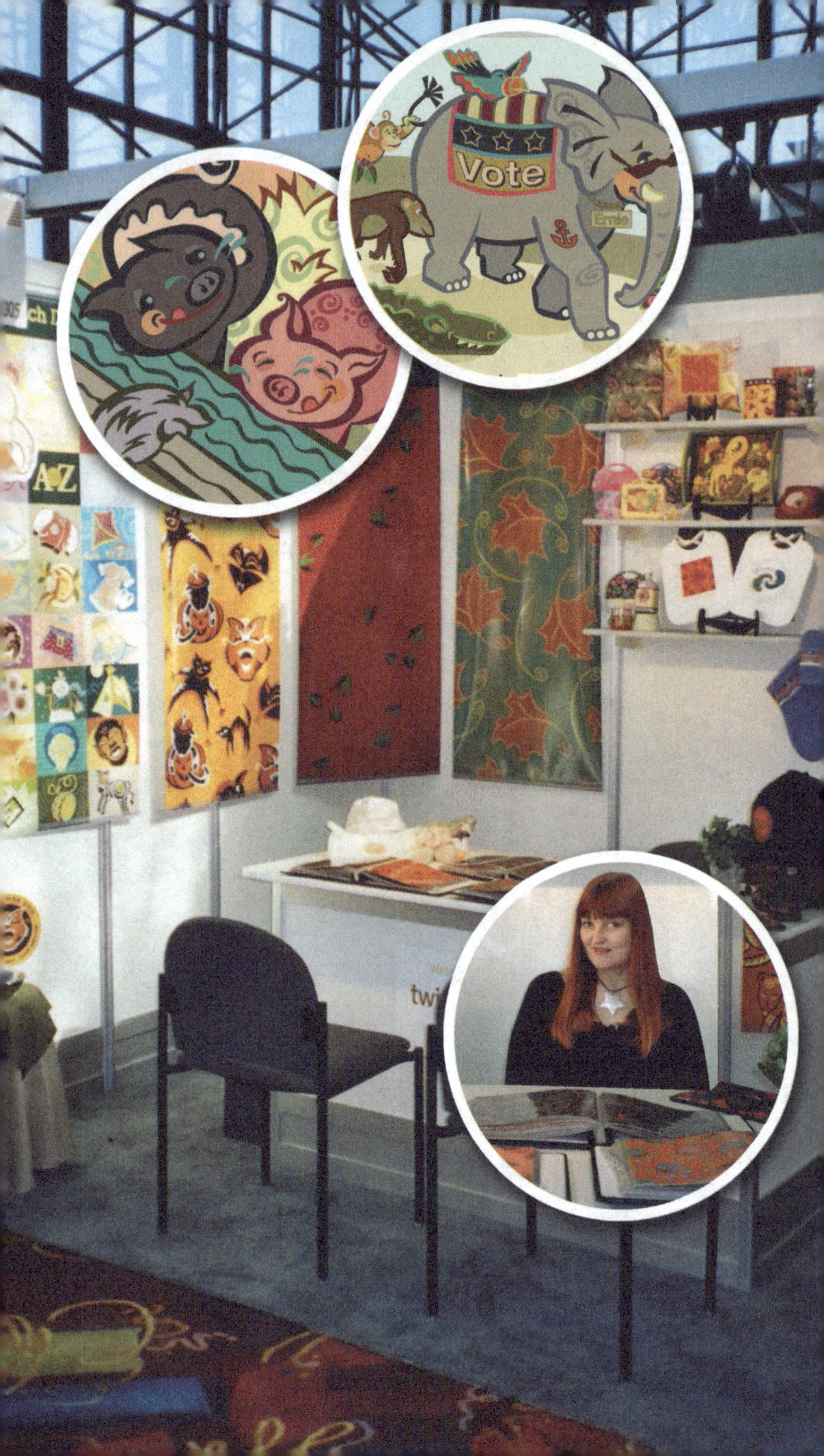
Vote

DESIGNING A LIFE

when beautiful becomes frayed
turned ordinary, accept that a magnolia blossom
will eventually fall from its branch

* * *

I created my first package design at age ten after hand-stitching an original design for Barbie. It was a tube of fabric that tied in the back or, if you will, an elegant evening gown. I'd seen the Barbie clothes in stores and noted that the manufacturer had stitched them onto cardboard before inserting them in the flat pink logo-encrusted box. "I can do that," I thought.

I attached the resulting monstrosity (read designer dress) to a piece of oak tag removed from a package of my mother's nylon stockings. With straight stitches, I sewed the dress to the oak tag and neatly lettered "Wonderful Evening" across the top of the cardboard in bold marker letters. I popped the resulting nightmare into a Baggie Sandwich Bag and stapled it shut. Voila. The wheel of my wheelhouse had begun to roll.

***

1973–1976, School Dazed at SIU: After a year of general studies at Southern Illinois University, I enrolled in the Commercial Art program earning an Associate degree. I audited boys, line dancing, and Tequila shots. As the end of my final year approached, we prepared for graduation and a gala event to celebrate our achievements.

Having dragged my 1,000-pound sewing machine to University, I was excited to make a life-sized "Wonderful Evening" gown for myself. My floor-length dress featured jungle animals around the bottom edge and across the bodice.

After dinner, the coveted Daniel Boza Award winner would be announced. Honoring one outstanding art student each year, I was sure my best friend, Sina, would walk elegantly to the stage in her autumn-striped gown, flashing her perfect smile, and return claiming not to deserve it. My name was called. It was me. I'm not kidding. It was me. It was a wonderful evening, and I had the dress to prove it.

After college, I moved back to Chicago, the city of my longing but not of my pocketbook, so my first adult home was a studio apartment on the Northwest side. The Ravenswood district was home to the Latin Kings, who kept watch over its neighborhood occupants. I was delighted to have someone looking out for me. They knew who I was, my car, and my building but never asked my name. It was like having a gang of big brothers.

Once, while standing by my car, blocked in by another vehicle and late for work, I was happy to see one of the Latin Kings walking toward me while motioning to another young man arriving on the scene. "Go roust the old guy from the first floor of the 1453 building," he called, "and tell him his presence is required."

1976–1978, Ross & Harvey Design: I felt confident arriving at my first job with an Associate degree in Commercial Art, and an award for outstanding student. I would soon be working downtown for one of my father's clients. I became Mark's apprentice, which he didn't need, until he met me. I made myself indispensable, doing everything my new boss didn't want to do—which most often meant production on what he would design—and did so with great enthusiasm. It was handwork back then. technical pens, T-square, and triangle to prepare the art for the printer. It included cutting up typeset galleys or graphics with an X-Acto blade and pasting it onto an illustration board with rubber cement. The resulting board, referred to as the mechanical, was then covered with tracing paper hinged along the top edge.

I was an apt production artist, but I couldn't wait to start doing design work. I had the honor of being asked my opinion occasionally, and soon, my boss asked me to jot down any ideas about the design of one project or another. After two years as an apprentice, it was time to make my magic happen.

1978–1983, Arnesen & Craddock Design Associates: I accepted a position as a Junior Designer at a studio that produced packaging for Kenner Toys. I'd ride the train downtown, circling Chicago's "loop" and hopping off near the Chicago River to walk the final leg to my office. During my five years there, I worked my way up to Senior Designer and was given two product lines of my own. I redesigned the Play-Doh line, which required art direction for photo shoots with models in diapers. Because kids photograph older, we often had to dip into the baby pool for models. On more than one occasion, I'd have to leave the Photo Studio, return to my office to repair the prototypes, or attempt to disguise the bite marks in the giant foam Play-Doh logo. Time was money, and there was no digital art back then. If we couldn't get it right during the shoot, the resulting 3" x 5" film transparency would need a costly revision. Had anything gone awry, we would need to pull a large color print from the film and send it out for retouching by an airbrush artist.

With "near-perfect" photographs in mind, tabletop set-ups required gloves, were framed with a Polaroid camera for layout, and dusted before shooting. I had to give the go-ahead to shoot film, and experience had taught me to say, "Not until we find the hair." There was almost always a single errant hair, no matter how many hair ties or baseball caps the photo assistant and I wore. I discovered that this final step, requiring no need for a re-shoot, often allowed for a game of chess before I needed to return to my office.

Next, I got the Alien toy package line to design when the movie came out. Kenner never produced the toys, but the prototypes for photography and the movie stills that I got to use were boss! It was determined, via parent focus groups, that the movie and toys were too scary for the little ones. In fact, Kenner wanted the Alien's head I used in the logo to not include teeth, so our airbrush artist made them disappear, leaving the terrifying monster to appear to have forgotten his dentures. Did they not understand that every teenage boy in America and beyond would want to collect absolutely everything "Alien?"

When presented at Toyfair in New York that year, buyers said, "No thanks," and I was left holding the duplicate mock-up of each handmade package design for the line. We had to make doubles for the exhibit in New York as they were delicate, and you never knew if the press-type letters would be scraped off in transit. Those second mock-ups helped pay a few bills when I was contacted by a collector years later.

During this time, I met my first husband, an artist, in Chicago, and we married a few years later. We moved first to an apartment in Chicago's Andersonville neighborhood and later to the Rogers Park area on the far north side. Thus began the "love equals heartbreak" scenario, perpetuating my subsequent abundance of moving from one home to the next. I worked as a **Freelance Graphic Designer from 1983-1987** as Starter Husband and I traveled from Chicago to the East Coast to seek our fortunes and fame as artists.

1987–1993, American Express Company: My husband and I settled in Hoboken, NJ, and I began work at American Express in New York, ferrying across the river daily to the ground floor in-house art department in the American Express Tower on the river's edge. Print and Multi-media departments served the employees of American Express who were responsible for selling their ideas to their boss and then to potential advertisers. My group produced printed materials while Multi-media created slide and video presentations.

Pre-computer during this time meant the production artists shared a bullpen filled with technical pens, illustration boards, and a hot wax machine for building the mechanicals headed to press. Each designer had a cubicle. Being a low rung on the ladder meant my cubicle was at the back wall. Creating sell sheets, ads, or handmade props to promote ideas brought to us by the team was enjoyable. My work life was moving smoothly, but my marriage ... not so much.

Along with problems at home were issues at work. Not the kind you might ever imagine, but, like all corporations, you must be promoted to prove your value. Each time I moved up the cubicle hierarchy, it meant more responsibility for work done by others and less creativity for myself. Based on my performance reviews, I became the Senior Art Director in year five of my employment. I was directing others to have all the fun, and it was not a gratifying outcome to have "excelled" to boss.

By this time, my starter marriage was toasted, burned, and scraped into a trash bin. I had moved to a studio apartment in Hoboken, and my best friend and I began causing all manner of trouble in town, as best friends must do. My carousing was shameless, and shots of Tequila became a staple, as was the smoking of cigarettes and general tomfoolery.

While out dancing and drinking one night, I met Don Brody, the world's funniest man. A musician playing in Hoboken as was requisite for musicians of that era, Don had seen me come in with a young man on several occasions. I was there by myself one night when he made his move. After ascertaining that I was single, he added my phone number to the band's mailing list, and the deal was sealed. We married in 1990, and Don became the stay-at-home parent when our son, Perry, was adopted.

I continued at American Express, the official breadwinner. And then it happened. The entire art department watched in horror as gigantic Macintosh computers were wheeled in and set up in each cubicle. We still had a usable corner of our drawing boards, but the learning curve was spectacular. My first "direction of art" in this new era was to require that all concepts first be presented to me as pencil sketches and later rendered digitally for the client. We artists went, kicking and complaining, but we went, and I was grateful to have learned a new tool.

I wanted to return to being a designer instead of a director, and received a job tip from a client at American Express. I was soon working in midtown, enjoying a new commute by subway.

1993–1996, Gruner+Jahr USA Publishing: Hired by *Parents Magazine* I became their Promotion Art Director in an art department of one, with my own little key to my own little studio, though able to call in freelance artists as needed. It was bliss, and I was there for three years, developing ideas to help sell the magazine to advertisers. One of the sales staff asked me to come up with an idea for him to approach a company that sold roller skates. I said, "How about a roller skate wheel?" My Latchkey-Kid status meant I knew how to make almost anything. I created a wheel, eight inches in diameter, that when turned, would reveal several pertinent facts regarding the magazine's readership through the stat-designated window. I didn't want to be too pushy, but I secretly hoped he would ask the advertiser to guess the stat before turning the wheel to reveal the answer. Come on, you know I'm right on this.

Toward the end of my time there, *Parents Magazine* acquired *Child Magazine*, and I became art director for both—without a pay increase. The family and employment universes aligned as Don and I, having recently bought a house in Weehawken, New Jersey, decided to adopt our second child. This would be my opportunity to be the mom that I had always hoped to be. Shortly after we decided to increase our family joy, Don found a job in sales at a record label in Manhattan, and I left my job to stay with Perry. Molly eventually arrived, and our family had become what I'd always dreamed it would be.

Tragically, some dreams don't last. Our newly

numbered family suffered greatly after Don passed away eighteen months after Molly was adopted. Thus began my longest run as owner of a graphic design studio staffed by one.

1996–present, Welch Design: For the next 28 years, I had two major Trade Association clients in New York who paid the bills enough that I could indulge in creative endeavors such as book cover design, logos, music packaging, online graphics, and working with start-ups and entrepreneurs.

Creating artwork for surfaces and textiles, I exhibited my illustrative patterns and designs at Surtex, the annual buyer industry event held at the Jacob Javits Center in New York. I was well-received, and most visitors to my booth were looking for something different, which I showcased in my Twistville Collection. I earned an apparel commission from Imagine Greenwear and another from Hasbro. Fisher-Price engaged me to create label decals for two *Little People* toy sets. Surprising jobs came from *Scott Foresman* and *McGraw Hill*. Both publishers wanted more imaginative illustrations included in their books for younger students. It was beyond what I could have hoped for, but "different" hadn't worked as well with parents, so buyers were looking for something different from different by the following year.

Currently living in northern California, I write, illustrate, and publish poetry books and children's picture books. My lifelong graphic arts work has informed my passion, an Indie Press called Welch Design Publishing.

I have designed a life full of important things. My personal portfolio includes a self-sufficient and creative child at its heart. It contains good fortune enough to have found the one person with whom near-perfection was achieved, if only briefly. My children have grown to be wonderful friends. I have erased my sharp edges and have learned to forgive. As in childhood, I am sometimes socially awkward, having recently hugged a friend in a bar without realizing she had a full wine glass in each hand. I have learned that it's not my job to be liked by everyone; I need only to present them with someone I enjoy being.

Keep this between us. I go to the Post Office at noon, knowing it will be filled with anxious humans who squeeze time into one-hour increments, hoping there's just enough left to do what must be done. I am another among others, discussing the new stamp designs and complimenting the day.

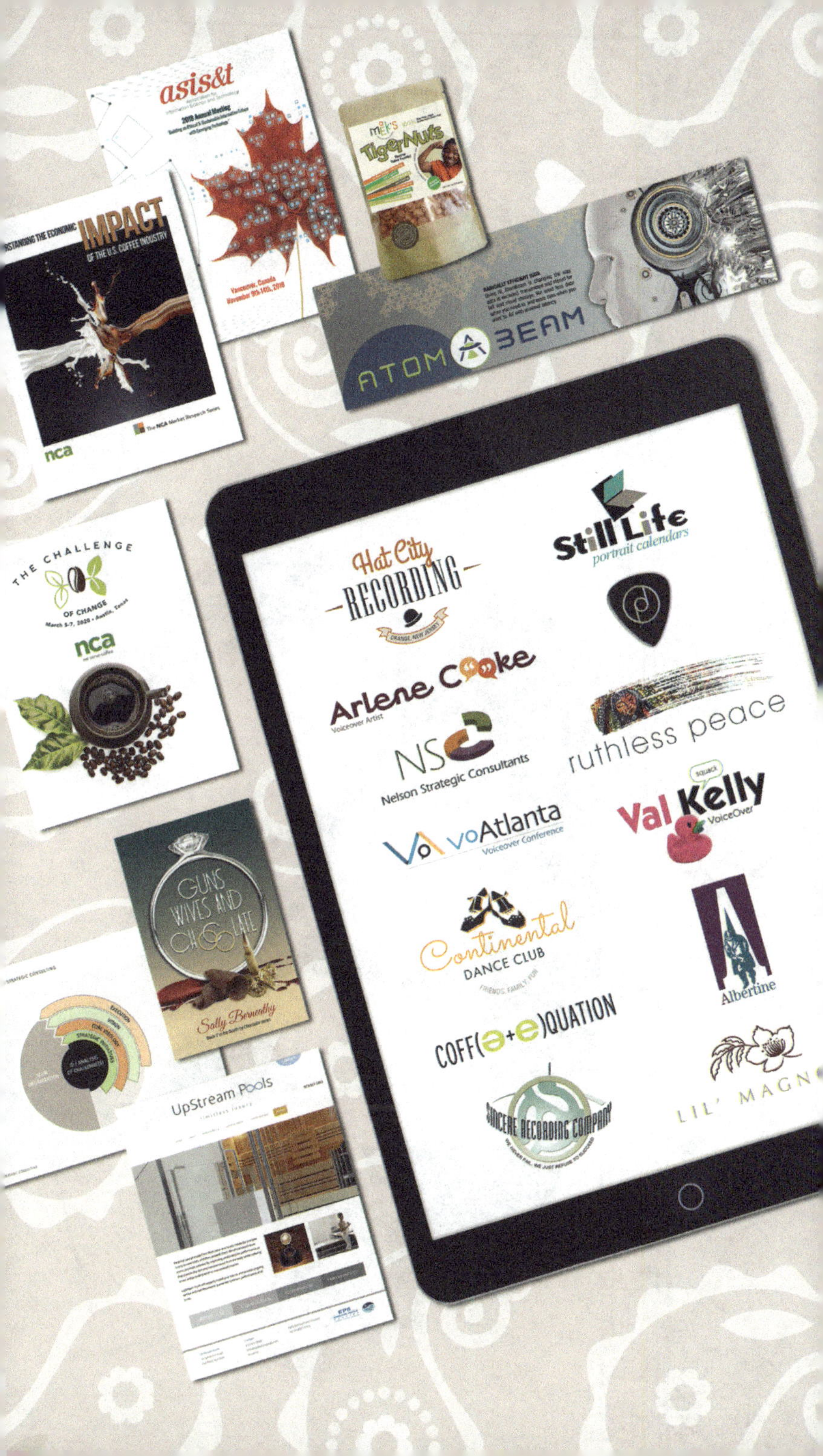

asis&t
Vancouver, Canada
November 9th-14th, 2018
IMPACT
OF THE U.S. COFFEE INDUSTRY
nca
The NCA Market Research Series
TigerNuts
ATOM BEAM
THE CHALLENGE OF CHANGE
March 5-7, 2020 • Austin, Texas
GUNS WIVES AND CHOCOLATE
Sally Berneathy
UpStream Pools
Hat City RECORDING
ORANGE, NEW JERSEY
Still Life portrait calendars
Arlene Cooke
Voiceover Artist
ruthless peace
NSC
Nelson Strategic Consultants
Val Kelly
squack
VoiceOver
voAtlanta
Voiceover Conference
Continental DANCE CLUB
Albertine
COFF(e+e)QUATION
SINCERE RECORDING COMPANY
LIL' MAGN

I thought that
when you walked
I thought that you
but you were on yo

Some h

"You make me feel
valuable."
all night long
moon

Why
and let me

SHORTEST MARRIAGE LONGEST LOVE

I touch the shining moon of your face,
speaking it all that it can hold in words
not yet invented

* * *

It seems that it was only a day from the moment I met my longest love until the hour that he passed away. In truth, it was 2,963 days exhaled as one long breath, beginning the minute we kissed after a Woody Allen movie on 8th Street, his hand finding the back of my neck. Voices sparked the Village as we turned our eyes to survey the concrete cornerstones of buildings that regret their inability to scrape the sky.

Within seconds, he played a song he'd written for me—before our first date—titled "All Night Long" (damn, that was bold). An instant after that, we stood in my kitchen, sampling something stove top retrieved and offered to taste from a big spoon. We moved into an apartment in Hoboken by midday and forever walked Washington Street, where Mr. Woods, a beloved local character, inspired Don to write a song that our children and friends still sing today. This song, "Old Mr. Woods," speaks of love having grown so full that there remains enough to share, even when we lose it. I feel this deeply.

The healing balm of Don's low voice and perpetual smile smooths my sharp edges. His comic good nature is pure magic, considering his years spent surviving childhood polio. I marvel at my good fortune from when he invited me to place my phone number on his band's mailing list (cheeky) to the honor of marrying this kind and funny person, forever sharing his wonderful family and storied life.

Our endless day continues with the arrival of our son, Perry, who leaves us breathless every time we try to speak. Don works hard to care for our son as I remain working, buoying and anchoring our world, arriving back to Hoboken early evening by ferry to the only man I would ever know as home.

Dinner finds us at a favorite local pub, with our

firstborn in tow, in a room swaying with music, friends, and laughter. Richie Havens can not resist playing peek-a-boo with our perfect child from the next table. "Pretend this is normal," I keep repeating to myself. A quick visit to swing the kid in the park, and then it's time to pack and move to the house we bought in the next town.

By evening, our daughter, Molly, arrives. I am grateful to become the work-from-home mom while Don rejoins the workforce, arriving home by bus as night falls. My heart quietly splinters as I watch, from an upstairs window, his post-polio steps falter. He reaches for support, plucking fence posts along the half block to our house. My soul becomes a worry doll placed under the pillow that I carry to lean against as we drive all night to surprise our Ohio family for Christmas. The baby and the 5-year-old are snug and sleeping in their winter car seats. I don't sleep. I still worry as I watch my husband's eyes lightly close while driving in the wee hours before dawn. I tell him that I want to drive for a while. "We're almost there," he says, "and I was just wetting my contacts."

Shortly after that, we shared laughter and dinner with Don's big family, who were surprised and happy to see us. After dinner, we gather in the living room to open gifts. Don seems tired, and heads to bed while I chat with the in-laws. We'd see most of them in the morning, as there was room enough to sleep the whole "fam damnly," as Don often said.

The day ends. It was a 2,963-day day filled with so much love, promise, and music that, to this day, it grows ever fuller.

At daybreak, he is gone. Those of us who love him, as well as those who've only met him once, live with his loss through all of our remaining days. The wind never whispers again or lightly lifts a mood. Instead, it sweeps us off our feet at times. It scatters our shatters, placing them in the arms of family and friends as we continue to relearn our lives.

* * *

We carry him forward, growing into each new day overflowing with playgrounds, work, schools, colleges, family, careers, music, and celebrations. Don must enjoy this if he can see us from wherever he has gone. We fervently hope that we have made him proud to watch us put one foot in front of the other as he had struggled to do all of his short-lived life. Sometimes we trip, sometimes we run, but always we move forward as he taught us to do by example. "Damn the potatoes, full speed ahead," he was known to battle cry.

I sometimes replay that long day, making a solid image of how I would have wanted it to resolve—a smile, a song, a painting, a timepiece gifted. Juice box contents cover our edges as bread bakes, healing us in warm slices.

Many miles separate my grown children and me. When we close our eyes at the end of our long days, we are thankful for the time we shared with our Don Brody, a man rarely without a one-liner and a fulsome grin. We find happiness in each other's miraculous lives.

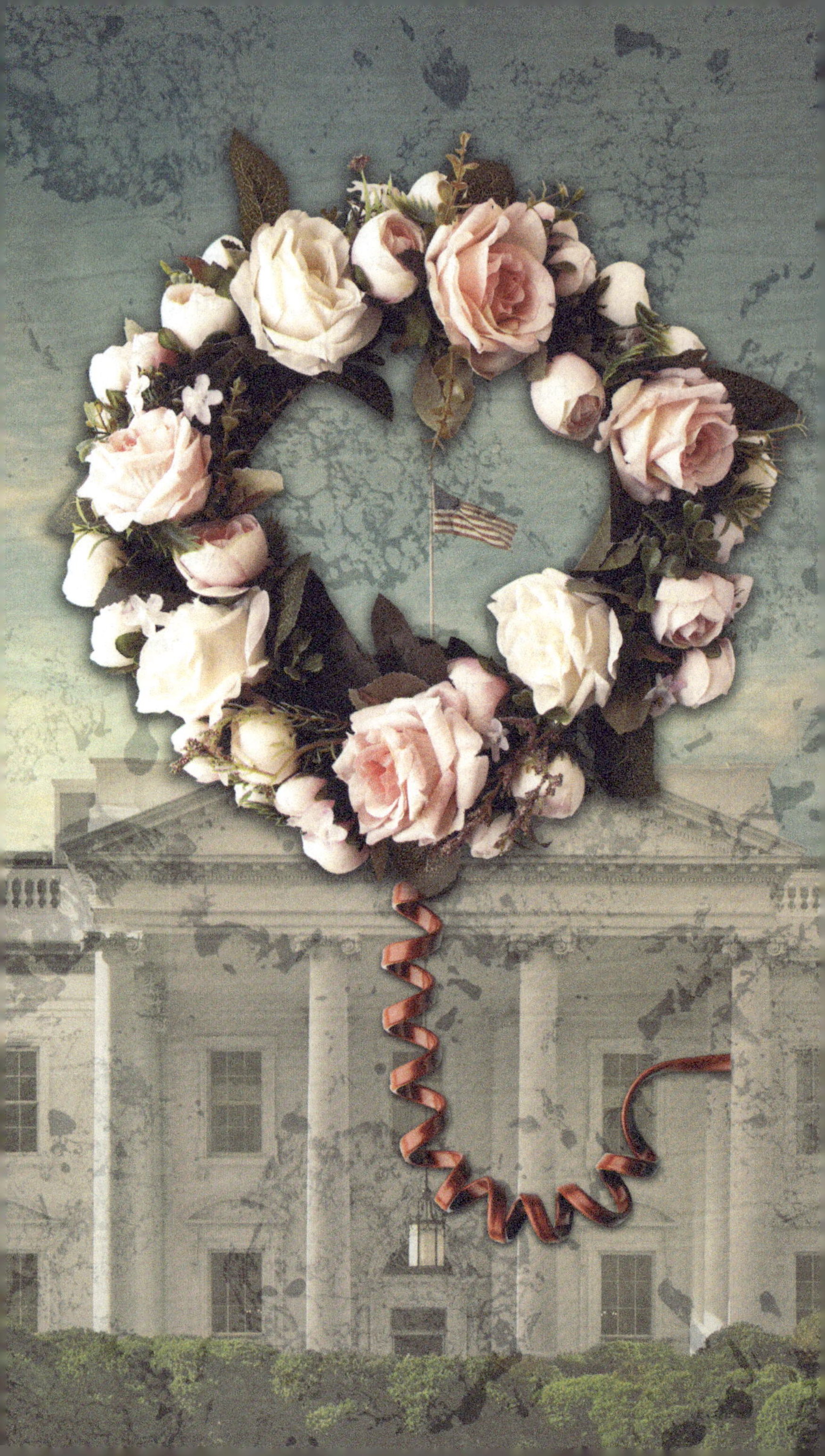

LIFE PRESERVERS

small treasures appear in shadow puppetry
ripple the glass in your pane
fall on your sidewalk, fall on the stones
just beyond your door

* * *

When my husband died suddenly at the age of 44, I sat on the kitchen floor, feeling our future lift away from my body. The present had become a series of unanticipated challenges. My husband and I had just adopted our second child 18 months earlier, and having promised both of their birth-mothers that there would always be a stay-at-home parent, I set about planning how to keep that promise.

Not only was I grief-stricken at the loss of my husband, but overnight, I had become a single mother of two small children with a mortgage and no income. Our families chipped in, and the community held several benefit concerts to help us restart our new lives. Local parents left bags of clothing and toys on our enclosed porch—even a toddler bed for the little one—and the town issued a check from donations made by the townspeople who heard our story. Our country was also there when we needed them. I set out to determine what our tiny trio might be eligible for.

The children were entitled to receive their father's social security benefits until age 18—which I was allowed to use to help keep us in our home. I restarted my Graphic Design business in the corner of my bedroom. I spent my days caring for the kids—cleaning, laundry, grocery shopping, cooking, playground—and my nights, after homework and baths were done, working too many hours to earn enough money to keep us going.

Those years were very difficult. I was so happy to learn of and qualify for the Earned Income Tax Credit. For those several years, while working round-the-clock to keep my family together and moving forward, I was not required to pay income taxes on the small amount I could earn. I never felt like a victim. I never believed I was taking a government handout but rather a hand-up. I knew I needed help and was grateful to have it. I knew I would eventually regain my footing, and I took comfort in knowing that the same help I received would be there for someone else when needed.

Today, my children are grown. My son, Perry, is a working musician and a third-grade Special Education teacher. My daughter, Molly, is quite a smartypants and is attending school to earn a degree in Health Information Technology. Her continued high grade point average qualifies her to be a paid Peer Tutor.

I am thankful to live in a country whose citizens have made a choice, through their votes, to care for the most vulnerable among us. I am proud to share this story about unexpected hope and the life preserver created to keep needy families afloat. America must remain the "village" that lit a match in my family's darkest hour.

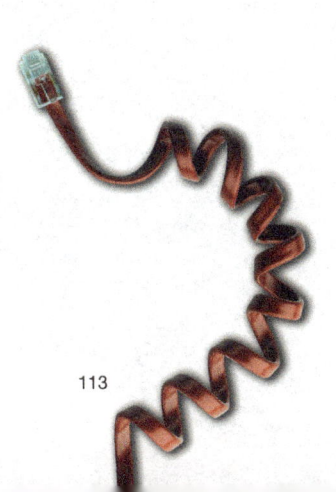

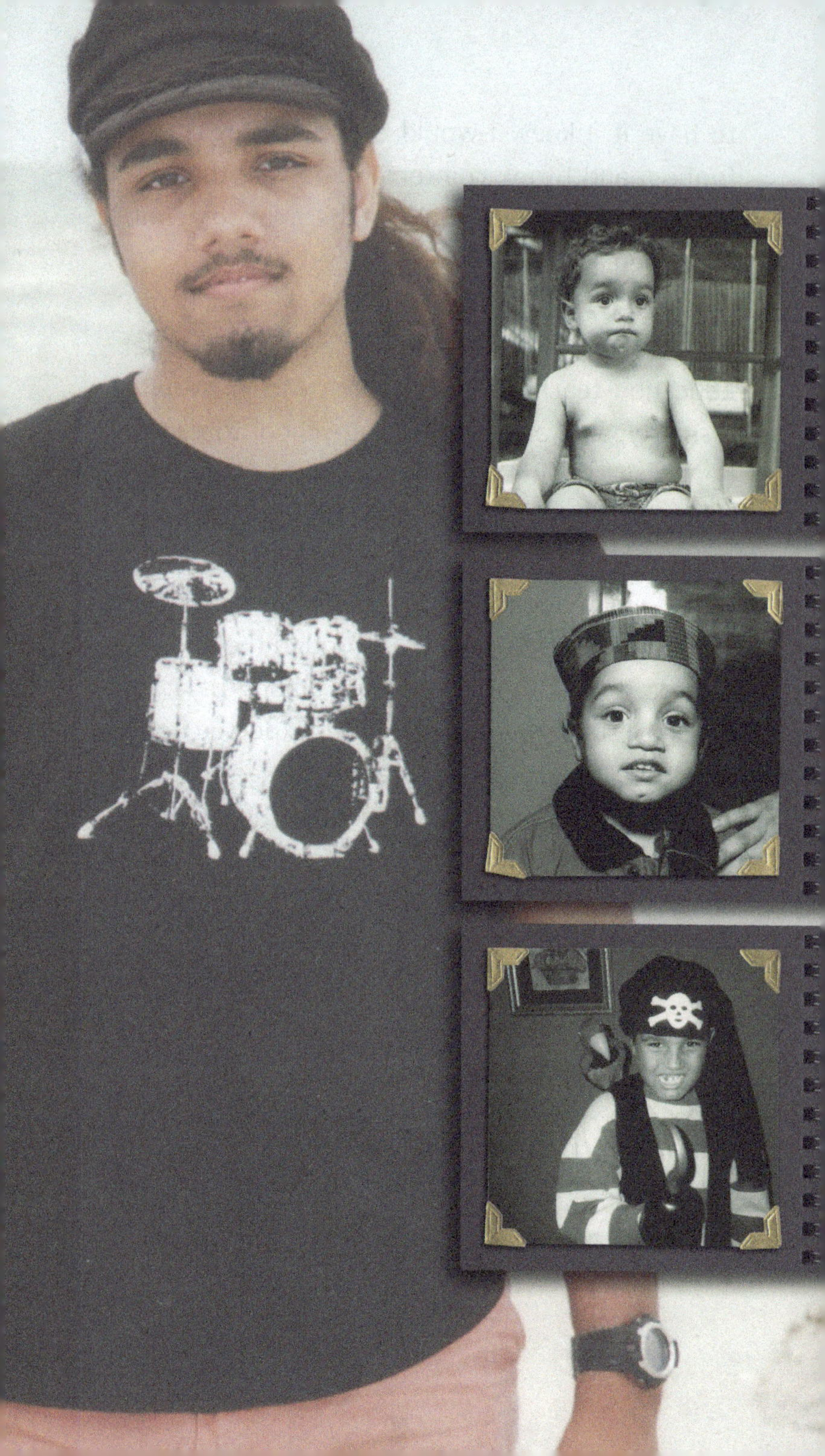

RAISING BABIES

I hold the horizon in a coffee cup
in a bed with no man's shape in folded landscape
I turn the morning in phrases of possible

* * *

Since it was my idea to promise each of our birth-mothers that there would always be a parent at home, I set about keeping my promise. Having spent my young years without the benefit of parenting, it was my way of balancing the scale, making up for my loss with my own children's gain. These kids were going to have as much of me as they needed.

Surviving would be the top priority. Having just lost my husband, my North Star, was more pain than I could carry at the time, so grieving would have to wait. Molly, having no concept of time, did not often ask where Daddy was. Perry, having been parented by Don for five years while I worked to support us, constantly asked when Dad would be home. It was nearly impossible to explain death to children so young. I remained honest and consistent. "Dad died, and everyone feels sad about that. Dying means that a person is no longer alive, and they can't come back," I'd repeat over and over, answering questions like "Can they eat," or "Can they walk." Still, the next time the phone rang, Perry would ask, "Is that Dad?" It hurt like a twister spinning through my internal landscape—knowing too well—that the worst of this was still in store for my children. My kids would eventually understand what had happened and fully grieve.

My young children required much attention, so I created a schedule. With Molly in diapers and Perry in Kindergarten, my day began very early. Once they were dressed and fed, we trundled off to drop Perry at school, just down the block. Playtime with Molly was always a pleasure, as she loved being read to and enjoyed serving me imaginary food from her toddler-sized kitchen that a friend had given us.

When Perry was in school and Molly was napping, I could call a friend or retrieve and sort the bags of clothes that regularly appeared on our porch. Occasionally, I had a minute to close my eyes and feel nothing.

After picking Perry up around 2:30, we'd head to the park where our friends often gathered. The other moms would converse on benches while I ran with my tiny crew—chasing, hiding, climbing, and sliding down slides. The other moms accused me of making them look bad. It was not my intention. I could not sit with them or hear the stories of their wonderful families or lazy husbands. I was also constantly afraid of being asked, "How are you doing." I would either be unable to start speaking or, once started, be unable to stop. So I ran instead.

Homework followed the park, and dinner followed homework. Baths followed dinner, and all of us would welcome some TV until bedtime. My son still chides me about their having to go to bed at 7 p.m. "I can hear Richie playing in the schoolyard!" he'd say. I had to go to work, so the best I could manage would be an extra book if it were short.

After reading to each kid separately, I'd sing a lullaby in the hallway between their rooms. These were our day-ins and day-outs with slight variations. An occasional 6th Birthday party would break up the routine. I was relieved to have a tiny toddler to hold onto while the other moms celebrated.

* * *

My load lightened up a bit when it became necessary to get help for Molly's speech impairment. I knew what she was saying, but no one else could understand her—and she would be four years old next year in public school Pre-Kindergarten. I visited our excellent public school to see what they might recommend. The speech therapist we met with wanted her to join a Head Start program in another school so that she could receive Speech Therapy through that school system.

So it was that little Molly, at three years old, would wait with me in front of our house for the little bus to pick her up. She traveled to the next town, where she would spend the entire day, arriving home around 3 p.m. She was so brave ... and so was I.

The therapist determined that she was not making any sounds in the back of her throat and Speech Therapy, which lasted for three years in total, solved the problem.

Our lives finally stabilized, and I eventually had the time to let Don's spirit take hold of me.

Sometimes, you aren't aware of how much you're holding in until it has a place to go.

* * *

File this under cautionary tale. Don and I had seen no harm in sharing stories of Santa Claus and the Tooth Fairy with our son. We could not know that Perry radically believed in everything joyous. So, there I was, realizing that his belief in such things had lasted longer than expected. I was hoping that some kid, you all know this kid—let's call him "The Spoiler" would at some point, sit him down on the playground and give him the bad news about these fantasy characters. It never happened.

I understand parents' good intentions to share "the magic" of their youth with this willing group of kids, but I was worried. Perhaps their children had not experienced the finality of actual death. My disclosure would prove catastrophic to my third-grader. Watching the hope in Perry's too-old eyes turn from joy to pain was almost unbearable. I knew this feeling and would never have wished it for my children. I was a soul-crushing monster and would never again deceive my children in this manner. This storybook tale, from our collective pasts, had failed like a practical joke gone wrong. When Perry finally came to the sad realization about Santa Claus, he asked, "What about the Tooth Fairy?"

As my daughter became more aware of Santa, it was interesting to see my son tell her that he is a make-believe character in a Christmas story but that some people pretend he's real because most grown-ups wish he were. Perry wouldn't let Molly go through that kind of pain—he was just a stellar young boy.

* * *

After several moves and missteps, Molly and I moved to California to enroll her in Vet Tech School. She later moved to Las Vegas for cheaper rent and another career path. Perry stayed in New Jersey, where his music and work were. It was so hard to make that separation. However, we now had the space and time to grow our best adult selves. I miss my kids, but we talk and visit often. I love California, and not so secretly hope that we will all end up out here together. For now, Perry and Molly are achieving beautiful things for themselves.

I have retired from Graphic Design and spend time writing, visiting friends, and dancing as the music moves me. I feel happy.

I feel Don's presence whenever the kids and I are together. I feel his lifelong commitment to trying harder, not complaining, and being joyful. I know that the kids, at my gentle urging, are starting to internalize Don's undaunted spirit. I hear his voice in night-middles. I imagine him whispering, "This single-parent wonder becomes you. I sing in your ear while you sleep, hoping to return your song."

In a sweet bit of irony, Perry's last visit here prompted a concerned call to his sister. "Mom is acting like a child," he said, "She's running off and forgetting things." He had, in fact, threatened to get me one of those toddler backpacks with a leash. I had to dive deeply into my behavior, wondering if I might need some "adult" supervision. I soon concluded that he'd never before seen me happy. And now that he has, I trust in his extraordinary capacity to feel happy for me.

My daughter is now 27-years-old. Only recently, she said that she'd had nightmares when she was about five years old and had come to find me. She told me she'd seen me at my desk at 3 a.m. and then went back to bed without disturbing me. I wonder how often she may have been looking for comfort in the middle of the night and had returned to her little bed. I picture her in mismatched jammies, having been worn by someone else's child, considering that my needs outweighed hers.

My son, now 32 years old, posted a photo of the three of us online. His opening line was, "If you knew our story, you'd be proud of us." I wept, feeling that I could not have let him down if he could come to that conclusion. He knew we did what we had always done, ending that same post with, "My little family has been through so much, but we just ... keep ... going. The only way we know how."

I'm so proud of my kids and can feel how proud they are of me. We made it to the other side of darkness with help from so many of our friends and family members. Whenever we gather now, we spend time at the ocean, redwood forest, or being totally badass at karaoke. I savor every minute we spend in each other's company.

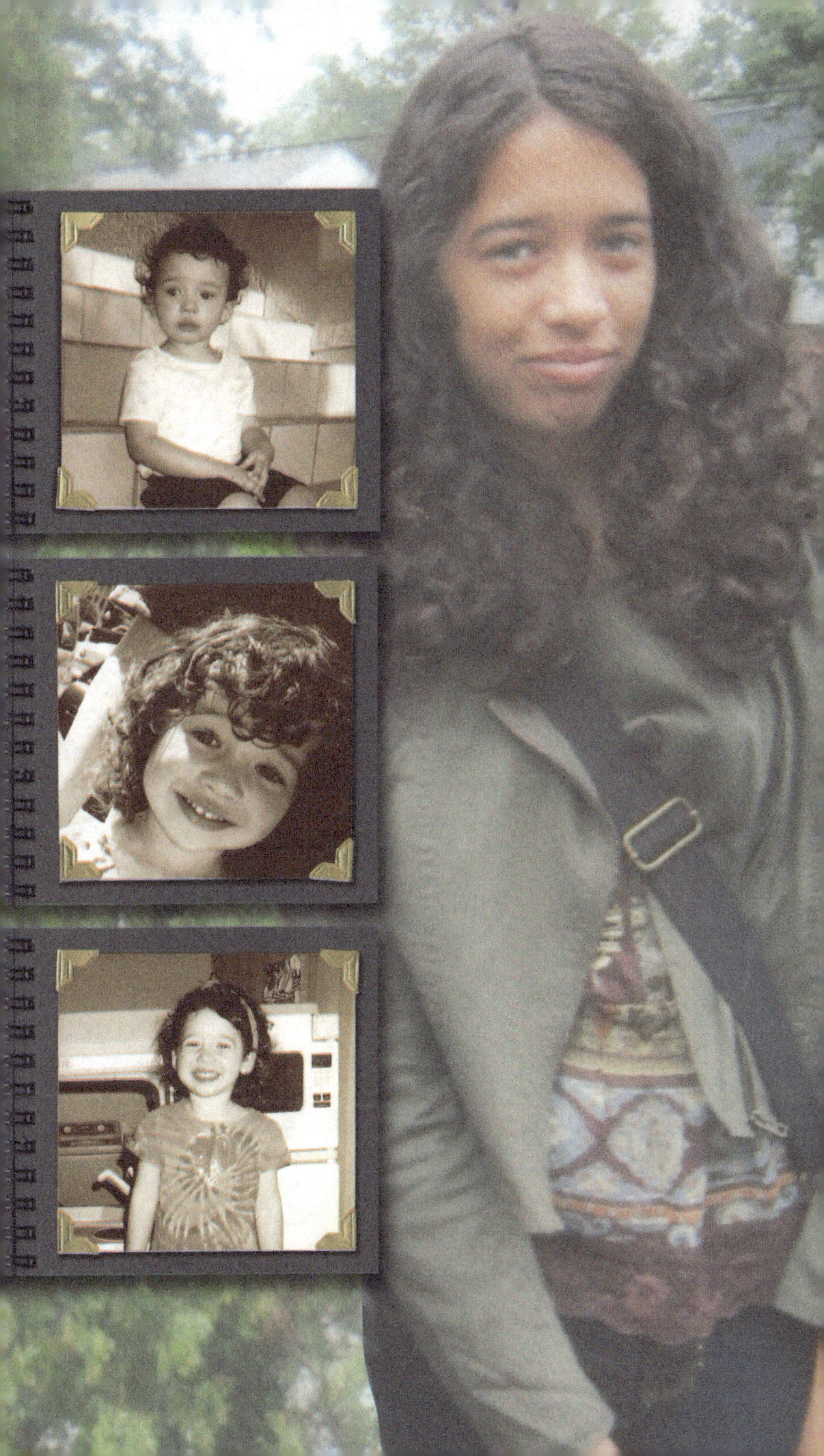

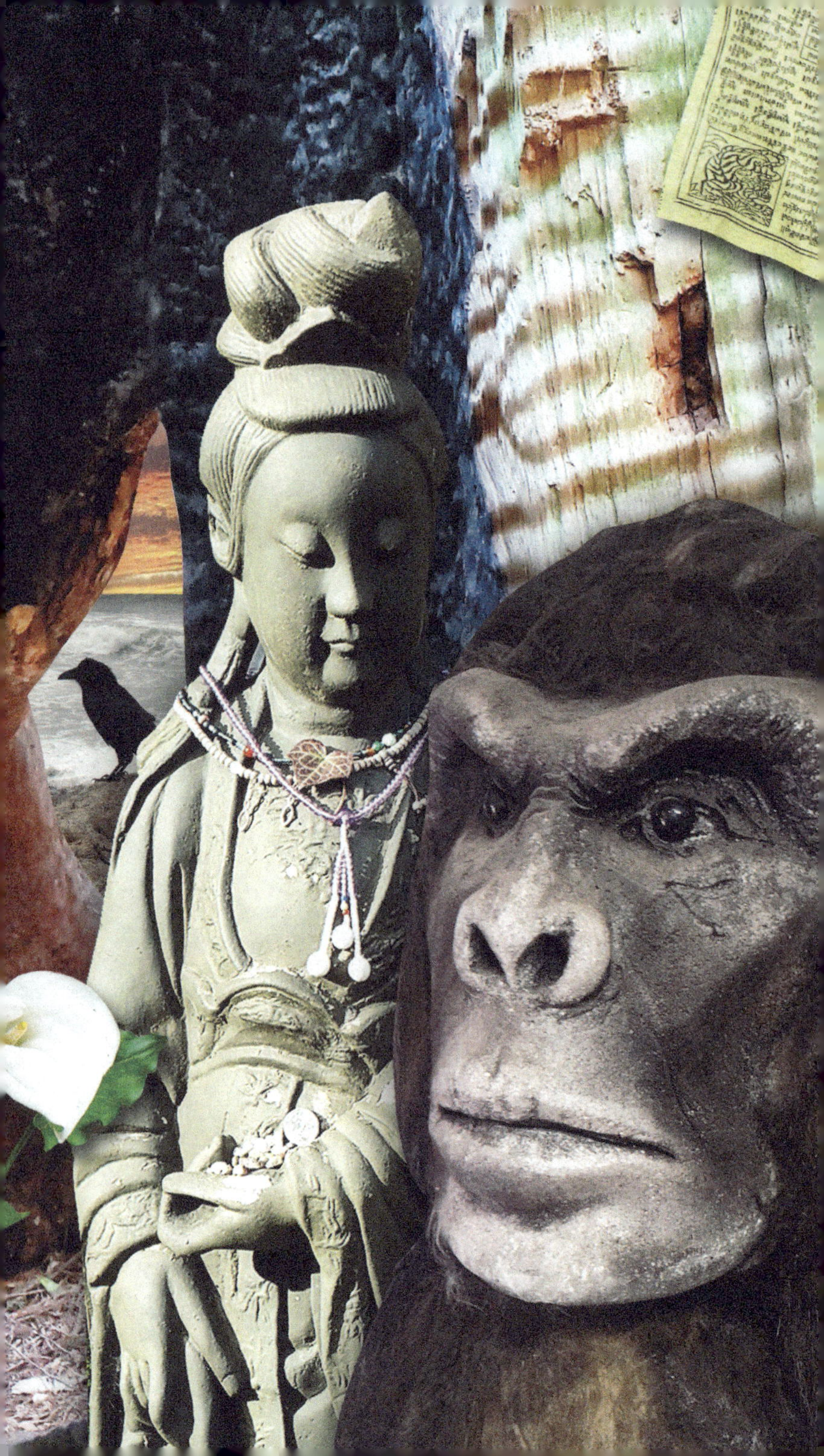

Sherpas

BUDDHA AND BIGFOOT

oddly surrounded by sunlit redwoods
folding him in shapeless, he entered not knowing
if it be home or hollow

* * *

The sun rose above my east coast ocean and would set below my new ocean on the west coast as the plane landed. My daughter, Molly, and I began a grand adventure that continues until this day, although now in separate states.

Circumstances in New Jersey were such that significant life changes were due for my daughter and myself. We were moving through life on autopilot, without much happiness or motivation to think too far into the future. Both of us had recent pasts that we needed to leave behind.

My son, Perry, was doing well in New Jersey. He had an apartment and work that he enjoyed as a paraprofessional in a school for kids with special needs. He was also well-known and loved in the music community, regularly gigging at local pubs, restaurants, and clubs. He had friends nearby and my ex-husband to count on if needed. Moving away from him across the country was a difficult decision, and I told him we would not do it if he objected. Because he is one of the kindest humans I've ever encountered, he wanted us to take our shot at finding something ... more. None of my moves seemed permanent; I wasn't entirely sure if I'd remain in my future home state after Molly, who planned to attend school in California, had graduated. I had a friend in Pacifica with whom we could stay until we had firmed up our plans. So, we loaded a truck with belongings and a car carrier with my little green Toyota Echo and boarded a plane.

I could only ever describe Pacifica as indescribable. This would be our temporary home until we could find apartments near where Molly would be going to school. I walked to the ocean almost every day. Pacifica's pristine beaches boast surfers of both human and canine breeds and a modern design Taco Bell that sits near the shoreline on Linda Mar Beach. Up Highway 1, a short distance, Rockaway Beach is home to giant boulders that witness the most incredible sunsets as giant black birds visit the rocks in search of food.

I continued to work remotely with my New York clients. My daughter's boyfriend arrived, and we found apartments in San Jose where Molly would attend Vet Tech School. We found a decent used car for her and were ready to launch.

***

In San Jose, I continued my freelance Graphic Design business for my East Coast clients, and recruited a few more clients by referral. We explored the area. Surrounding us were beaches, amusement parks, museums, music venues, lush gardens, and redwood forests. We checked out Alcatraz, the strange Winchester Mystery House, and all that San Francisco had to offer.

In Felton, California, the Henry Cowell Redwoods State Park is a place of historic beauty covered in damp moss. Smelling of dirt and wonder, some of its centuries-old trees have fallen and lay feeding the forest floor with their rotting. In this place, at this time, a kind of peace entered my soul. The dappled light on the forest floor spoke of past, present and future, of grace, of coming home.

Near the redwood forest, a small museum is dedicated to one of the local celebrities. The Bigfoot Museum and its curator stand ready to regale visitors with stories and photographs, movie reels, and audio recordings of this larger-than-life creature. Carved wooden statues that flank the exterior of the tiny museum feature the entire Bigfoot family, including a Bigfoot child (Littlefoot?) hoisted onto his father's shoulders. Bigfoot memorabilia, news stories, and toys fill the walls of this tiny ode to a giant life imagined or believed. I've visited here many times, not caring whether the stories of Bigfoot are true or not, but only to feel how deeply the museum creator believes they are. I have found myself day-dreaming about taking over the museum should it be faced with closure if only to keep this one man's lifetime of belief from falling silent in those hills.

Not far from Felton, the Land of the Medicine Buddha in Soquel features a 100-acre Buddhist retreat offering meditation and workshops. Open to the public; visitors must remain relatively quiet as they tour the trails dotted with Calla Lilies and Buddha sculptures. Prayer Wheels, temples, and other sacred sites mark the miles of pathways. Makeshift shrines are found in hollow trees where visitors have placed photographs, art, poetry, and jewelry in honor of loved ones passed. The quiet is disrupted only by the sound of creeks and winded leaves. It's easy to see why the sentient life forms in California—and Midwestern heathens such as myself—are equally drawn to such peaceful enlightenment. In this area of California, I feel as close as ever to believing in anything I could not touch. Forest, legend, and religion unite to fill the "miracle" placeholder that had remained waiting, heart and head, for confirmation of existence.

***

My son, still in New Jersey, continues to find his best self by teaching and creating music. He has grown unique, kind, and brilliant (or so says his Mom). I am ever grateful that Perry can visit California often and enjoy this peacock of a state opening its Technicolor tail, and flaunting the beauty of its land and people. Being a musician, Perry usually plays a gig or a jam in the area, meeting more people than I have during my years here. He's a personable young man, and everyone he meets looks forward to his return.

After the pandemic, my daughter and her boyfriend, Jake, needed cheaper rent and moved to the Las Vegas area. I am fortunate to have one of my brothers living across town and the other two residing upstate. I also have nieces and nephews in the area, so holidays are always opportunities for family events. Most of the time, however, I'm on my own, spending my time as I did when I was young, creating.

Before the plane touched down at San Francisco International Airport those long months ago, I felt like I'd lived in black and white. That first evening, the sun would set in visible and felt colors. There would soon be loud music, quiet forests, and people to meet who would become friends. I felt myself open like a flower, having turned my face toward the sun.

I feel happy here, at home, and generally at peace. I sometimes think about my childhood, picking up rocks from the beach while stepping over dead fish. I love that child, and, in most ways, I am still that kid, simply living with the volume turned up.

I often think of my little family along the river that separated New Jersey and Manhattan. How hard we worked to overcome grief by moving forward as best we knew how. I think of my ocean in New Jersey, where my children and their father shoveled the sand or dozed under an umbrella while I walked over crushed seashells broken and then hurled upon the beach by brutal waves. I carry these pieces of the past into the future of my new home, my new ocean.

I will probably move again as my children tether themselves to adult homes of their own. Somehow, we will find a way to all be closer to each other. I don't know how far or where that will be, but I do know that Buddha and Bigfoot are now permanent passengers along for the rest of this wild ride.

Says U.S.
Recession
it's going
to change
the face of
the world."
A Coronavirus Great Awakening?
Lack of basketball, baseball prompts
Number of infections
across country pass
China's count, New
York remains epicenter
featuring
to buoy
offering
Some sides
COVID-19 rules make

I DIDN'T LEARN THE UKULELE

we removed our masks,
the ones to protect us from the virus
but not from losing ourselves

* * *

Announced by the CDC in early January 2020, the worldwide COVID-19 pandemic claimed its first reported case in the United States on January 24. By St. Patrick's Day, the World Health Organization had declared a global health emergency.

    Theaters, restaurants, shopping centers, churches, sporting events, schools, and non-essential businesses were closed until further notice. Grocery stores operated as best they could, but the shelves were often bare. Hospitals remained open, becoming makeshift morgues as the death toll rose. The Stock Market crashed, losing 37% of its value between February 12 and March 23,[1] rivaling the Great Depression.

My children and immediate family survived by getting vaccinated as soon as vaccines were available, masking even outdoors, and sheltering in place. There were many avenues that the government, under President Trump, could have chosen to combat the virus. They decided not to, and the President, at one point, joked that the CDC should "slow the testing down"[2] because it was making his numbers look bad. I will leave much of this to history and focus on my own experiences during this time.

My first day of sheltering in place began slowly, uncertain, dreamlike. My cat usually slept in her cat bed but would sleep against my side all night. She seemed to sense my anxiety and wanted me to know that she was there for me. I had no choice but to do everything I could to help slow the deadly virus. I followed the rules and hoped that others would, too, not only for their sake but also for everyone they came in contact with. Disappointingly, millions did not.

I watched the news for signs of the virus slowing, but it would be years before "normal" returned. It was unfathomable to watch entire cities shut down. San Francisco, once a vibrant city and tourist mecca, had ceased functioning, as did most locations worldwide that relied on tourism. Our poverty-stricken and homeless populations were the first to succumb to the disease. Our vulnerable persons, already with health problems, did not fare well.

It was clear that my son's April flight to California would be canceled. I didn't even want to think how long it would be before I could put my arms around him, but I was glad to know he was keeping himself safe in New Jersey. My daughter and her boyfriend, Jake, were nearby for the first year and then moved to Las Vegas when a logical window opened. Unable to work, they needed cheaper rent. I could only bid them farewell and vow to see them soon. We kept close tabs on each other, but my fear for them was within each waking hour.

My Graphic Design Business quickly dried up as all meetings and events moved to online formats. When I finally accepted that we were all in this for the long hall, I needed to have a plan that would inform my future. President Trump held a press conference suggesting that we "enjoy our living rooms"[3] which was rich. My living room had a bed in it, but we Latchkey Kids knew what to do once we'd locked the door from the inside. I would learn things, make things, and look after my family and anyone else I might come in contact with.

I ordered a ukulele. Having threatened to learn a musical instrument for years, it seemed a good time, and this particular instrument could arrive by mail. It sat for a long time, as did I. It longed to be touched, but the ukulele would have to wait. I decided that it was time to explore my lifelong passion for writing. Some days, it was hard to get out of bed, but on good days I would take an online writing course. Opting first for Anne Lamott and David Sedaris video tutorials and then poetry workshops as I came across them. It felt so wonderful to, once again, walk this creative path as I had in high school when I worked on the staff of our literary and poetry publications. The world began to slow-spin a new life for me.

During the pandemic years, I added to my collection of written and illustrated children's books published under my publishing brand. After that, I wrote poetry night and day, spilling words into spiral notebooks at an alarming pace. Lined pages become published books advertised on Facebook and sold on my website and Amazon. It soon became apparent that I was saving and rebuilding my own life. Through my writing, I felt sorrow for the little kid I was, melancholy for my lonely teenage years, and pride in the time I spent learning a career in college. I'd had a successful career as an artist and many unsuccessful love relationships. All were grist for the poetry mill.

My marriage to Don, adopting our children, buying a home, and filling it with music and toddler's toes being gobbled—all covered in my poems. In writing about the devastating loss of Don and the subsequent years of struggle as a single parent of very young children, I was studying my own master class of life. Much of my core truths had not changed over the years. I gave myself the break that I'd not often been given. I would forgive myself for the times I'd been resentful or angry. I'd forgive those I'd encountered who often did not deserve it.

The pandemic did not help me understand how delicate life is. I'd witnessed that so often that I could write a book (wink). It taught me that we are an intricate lace of people and places and are responsible for weaving ourselves whole enough to maintain our delicate combined existence. We need each other and depend upon each other's agreement to be part of the human race. I emerged from the pandemic a stronger version of that woven human thread.

I'd discovered through writing that I was already pretty good, to begin with; I only had to convince myself of that. I would permit myself to see all the colors, hear all the sounds, and feel the warmth of every hug once the world began hugging itself again.

That ukulele sits on a closet shelf, reminding me of the quiet possibilities in the hurricane's eye, the birds' gentle circling within the swirling dark despair. That ukulele can hold a tune just a bit longer while I act childishly with my kids, enjoy the weirdness of my family, and find love among my friends. It can placeholder my return while I discover the wild beauty on the trail, at the ocean's edge, and on the dance floor.

---

1. Liz Frazier, "The Coronavirus Crash Of 2020," Forbes, February 11, 2021 (accessed March 13, 2024)
forbes.com/sites/lizfrazierpeck/2021/02/11/the-coronavirus-crash-of-2020-and-the-investing-lesson-it-taught-us/?sh=680e967b46cf

2. Kevin Freking, "Trump suggests US slow virus testing to avoid bad statistics," The Associated Press, June 20, 2020 (accessed March 13, 2024) apnews.com/article/virus-outbreak-donald-trump-ap-top-news-joe-biden-tulsa-476068bd60e9048303b736e9d7fc6572

3. Emily Goodin, "' Enjoy your living room.' Donald Trump tells Americans NOT to travel as he confirms domestic restrictions can't be ruled out and says he is 'NOT happy' with people defying social distancing guidelines," Daily Mail, March 17, 2020 (accessed March 13, 2024) dailymail.co.uk/news/article-8122655/Enjoy-living-room-Donald-Trump-tells-Americans-NOT-travel.html

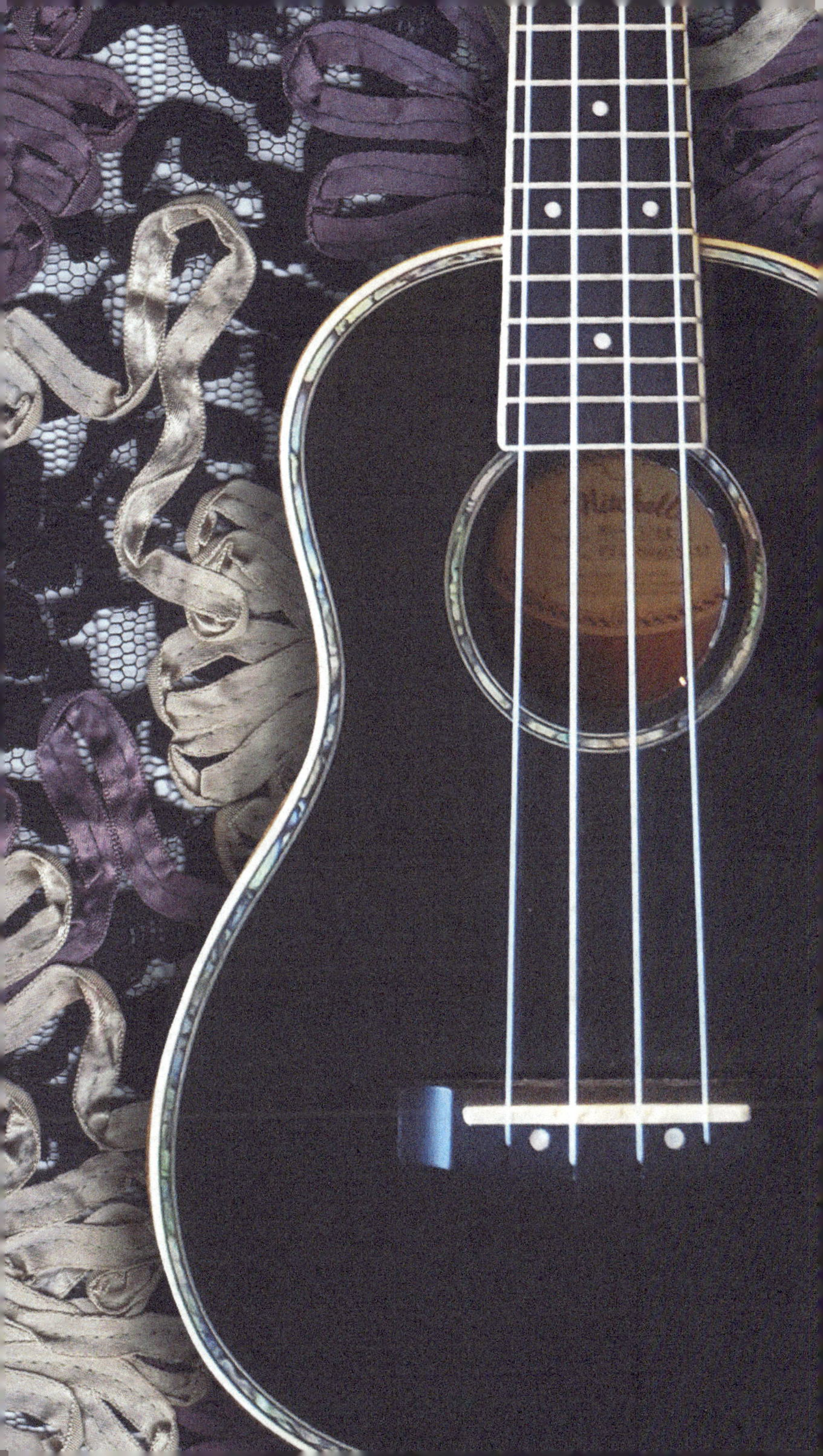

LIBERTY
IN GOD WE TRUST
2022
D
IN GOD WE TRUST
LIBERTY
HOW YOU DOIN'
IN GOD WE TRUST

ADULT DATING

*you are a rough blanket on top of smooth skin,
a disappearing act whose magician can not recall
how to recall you*

* * *

With children growing and thriving, or at least surviving, having a partner to share some of life's leftover sweetness with would be nice. Sure, time had pummeled most of my hope for this, but there was always room for a "Dime Surprise." When I was growing up, our local market offered everything grownups would need on the daily—coffee, milk, bread, beer, and cigarettes—and the best thing that 10 cents could buy. We kids would line up our pennies on the counter, hoping to find a wonderful surprise inside a sealed envelope. Every envelope was unique, filled with expired edibles and assorted junk having fallen from ripped-open packages on store shelves. We would excitedly empty our envelopes on the concrete outside the store, revealing our gum or candy along with something that would never have been guessed by observing the envelope's exterior. It might be a whistle, comb, tattoo, puzzle, pencil sharpener, or nail file. Adult dating would be fun, I'd hoped, full of surprises and all that was needed to build a solid foundation using decades of experience found in our envelopes—kindness, compassion, comics, more than one tattoo each, and the truth grown wise through the years and within our hearts.

It has been more like dancing in a minefield. We, the singular persons, armored in past harms, twirling our partners through exploding ex-wives and sneak appearances of a past lover's forgotten undies. It would prove challenging, but I was from New Jersey, damn it! Navigating our little histories and sad mysteries would be a cinch here in California, the land of old hippies and meditation. That was some lousy thinking on my part. Finding a person over the age of 60 who had not been severely scarred proved impossible. If we laid our collective shrapnel wounds end-to-end, they would stretch cross-country and back, including a stop at the Grand Canyon, smelling of oceans and failure. Surely we can save ourselves by saving each other, I think—be the poultice, the restorer of faith, the last bandage ever needed.

I have discovered that how one recovers from past relationship trauma is much like the two types of cops having been shot on a stakeout. One tells the surgeon that he doesn't want to see the bullet that nearly robbed him of his life, his family, and the world in which he had so much work left to do. And then there's the cop who wants the bullet preserved as a reminder of how fragile every single day is. She considers the bullet a living embodiment of her value. She has it cleaned of bloodstains and places it in a small jewelry box in her top drawer. Some days, she may look at the bullet, turning it over in her fingers, shaking her head at its weightlessness in her palm. She feels the pain, remembers the healing, embraces herself in newly discovered love. She is intensely aware of how close she came to losing it all and vows to respect every day that she is alive. She promises to serve and protect while knowing that life is a single heartbeat away from death. I am this cop. I am a keeper of "bullets," each one that landed or grazed, and I am committed to honoring my one sacred life by reviewing them from time to time.

*I offer below a few things
that I have learned while dating
in my "golden years"*

1

If your partner does not snore, consider giving them at least two additional strikes, on top of the traditional three, before they're out.

2

Make sure that your intended is "As Advertised." Refrain from accepting a stand-in for the real deal. They may reveal a side of themselves that you'd never have imagined. Remember how you felt after waiting two weeks for delivery of the giant clock radio you ordered online, only to pull out a clock radio pencil sharpener from the tiny box received? It's like that.

3

You may never find the "love of your life," but a close second is worth the effort. Understand that a third or fourth place is a gamble. Only you can throw the dice, close your eyes, cross your fingers, and whisper a plea for "7" or "11." It may be essential to remember that if you roll "boxcars," there is only a 1/36 (or 2.777%) chance that they will show up again.

4

If a significant other lies to you about something important, you must assume that they have lied to you before and will do it again if given the opportunity. Please don't give them that opportunity.

5

If you can't believe how lucky you are to have found such a terrific person, check yourself in the mirror. Consider that they may be the lucky one.

6

If your partner continues to demand that you not interrupt when they're speaking and then rolls their eyes in the middle of what you're saying, they've already decided that your opinion is worthless because it does not align with theirs. This type of person cannot make space in their life for anyone but themselves.

7

Rely on your intuition if in a museum after closing—with no decent docent to explain why Michelangelo's "David" was not the perfect male specimen—but was, in reality, a little dick.

8

Dear Cinderella or Cinderfella (we see you Jerry Lewis), there is no glass slipper that fits only your foot. There are only uncomfortable brown shoes, with arch support, in the wrong size because your feet have shrunk. They slide back and forth when you walk, and callous your heels. Still you must choose to attend the ball.

9

If anyone raises their voice to you or calls you names, don't think that they will change because your love for them is so strong. They won't, and you deserve better.

10
Be the first and last line of someone's love song.

BONUS
Leos and Scorpios, not so much.

* * *

I still hope for a safe and comfortable home with a garden doused in rosy hues and smelling of optimism. I would love to find a partner with whom to share laughs and dreams in equal measure. I imagine how wonderful it would be to hear music in the yard, our medley of children and grandchildren jamming on pots and wooden crates. The little ones pounding out the beats of their hearts, loud and strong, for the neighbors to "enjoy." If that never happens, I will continue to believe that believing in believing is enough.

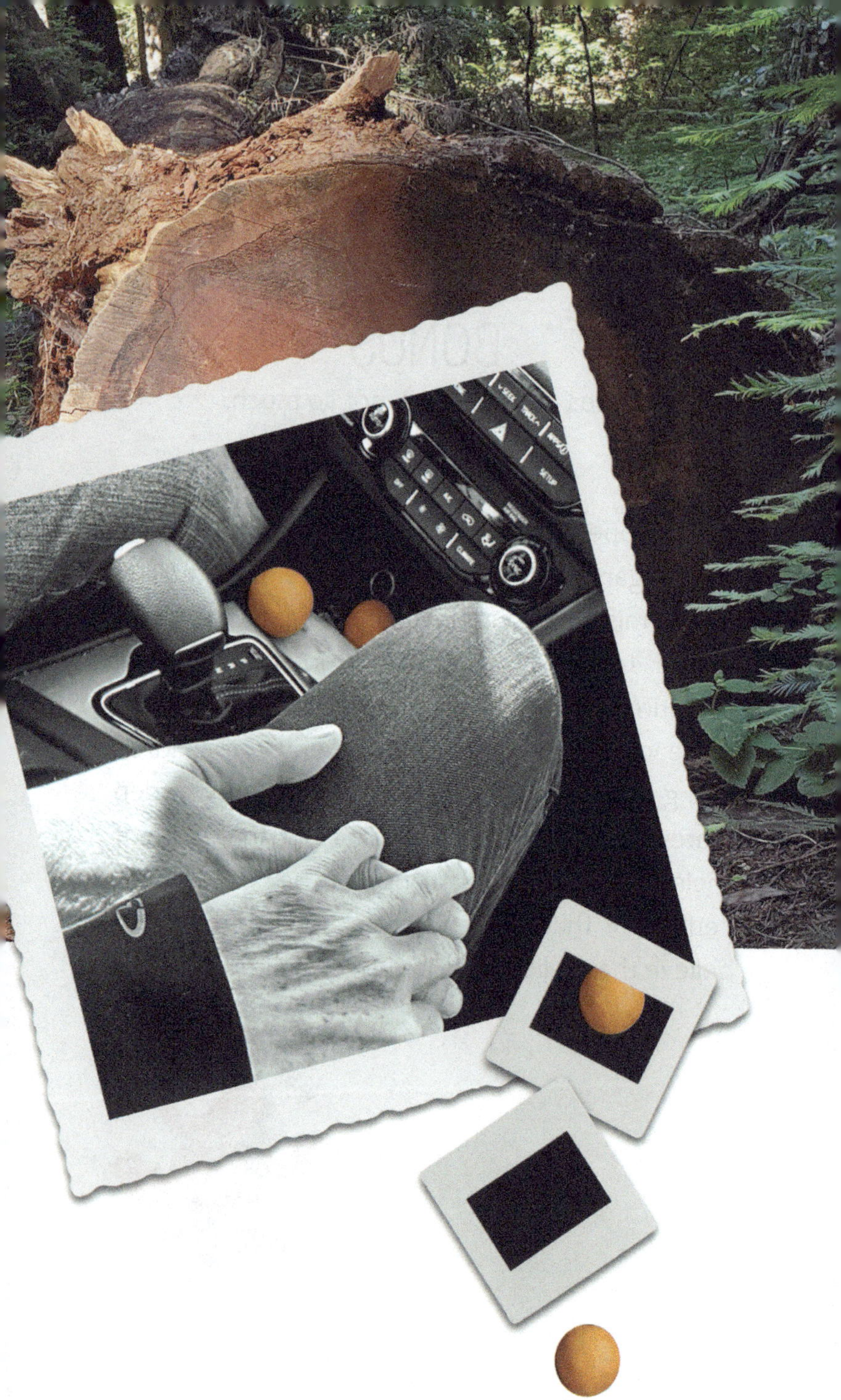

MISSING WHAT'S MISSING

a laying down, a picking up in one smooth action
she employs a frugality of emotion
a having and losing of love in the same tear

* * *

I got dressed this morning. It was not an ordinary morning. It was the fourth morning of the break-up morning. It was not sunny. But the light came in too early, burning my eyes with the sorrow they held. It was time to dress.

A shower would be wasted. Socks from yesterday would be OK. My closet dazzled me, as it always does, with pattern and color, so much of which I spend no time on matching. It suits me to clash, wear this armor that may cause passersby to turn sly a lipstick mouth or raise an eyebrow.

I chose the snazzy pants, the graphic tee, and more necklaces than any one person should wear at one time. I don't worry about fitting in. I never have, and I wasn't about to waste time on that now. I tattoo my body in fashion-weird and love the feel of it adhering to my legs and chest. It is a second skin that tells my story. "I am the one you will love," it says, "charming and witty, a rare gem."

Four days have passed since I was not what he wanted. I look out my window to the mountain in the distance. It is only fitting that this majestic, foggy, and immovable object would witness our leaving each other.

* * *

Four days prior, the all-powerful mountain seemed to watch us. It's green sides thanking the sky for more damn rain than any one state should be allowed. I was grateful for its tree-covered command of our attention as we sat on my porch, chairs almost touching— sunlight-rimmed coffee cups bubbling in reflected glints of light. We spoke of shade trees and music. We said our heartaches in the daylight so they would not permeate the shadows. We'd not been together for very long, him and me.

"Are you happy," I ask, "or has life broken you with its lessons?" He doesn't read my poetic query as actionable, so I attempt a second conversation launch. "How do you feel about us?"

The neighbor's TV is too loud. Dogs are barking, and the children downstairs demand attention from their weekend father. Dad's girlfriend quickly produces art supplies to quell their shrill voices.

I can hear my love's heavy breathing, his hopelessness, reaching for words he doesn't want to say. I know that it's over. I know I must throw this floundering fish back into the river, set him free. But here we are for now, on my porch, drinking coffee and not talking about the weather, politics, or families and friends. Instead, we speak in eyelashes rising and falling in time to a light breeze.

It was familiar. In vain, I attempt to lift heavy feelings from a light man who seeks to be released from the hook and thrown back to swim another day. "The sun is my favorite star," I offer, "because its surface is in constant motion that we can't see." He thanks me for coffee and leaves. We don't speak again.

**

I've run this play too often in different towns and states. I've had this same conversation with different men, patiently waiting for me to figure out that we've hit the end of our future and have already begun living our past. The question deviates depending on the man. Sometimes, "So, how's it hangin'?" is enough to pry words from an apathetic heart.

I would be like a missing puzzle piece, fallen from a beautiful landscape. I dislike leaving the puzzle incomplete, but I am satisfied with the fact that his picture is also now missing something.

I spent post-break-up weeks unlearning what I had come to know about whichever "him" it happened to be at the time. I unlearn the flowers and phone calls, forgive the kissing in public and sleeping late. I write our romantic obituary on scraps of paper retrieved from the recycling bin.

> Dear friends, today we have witnessed a solitary red beet slide off of a tipped plate. It's natural to feel as blue as the berry stain on your mother's favorite blouse or as purple as the bruise hidden under a flannel shirt. All colors have, this day, fallen from the edge of an emotional cliffhanger. We patiently await the rise of another rainbow.

I review the regrets available and plan a path forward as I've done many times. I leave the battle that began with open hearts and ended with closed doors—knowing that the lack of that one last word would always be lacking. I allow myself the necessary exhausted exhale. I remind myself of Mazlo's Hierarchy of Needs. There's a reason that "self-actualization" sits atop the pyramid, preceded by "esteem" and "love." It is good to remember that our version of who we are ultimately matters beyond what seems forever missing. I find myself still spending love freely, without concern for the deficit.

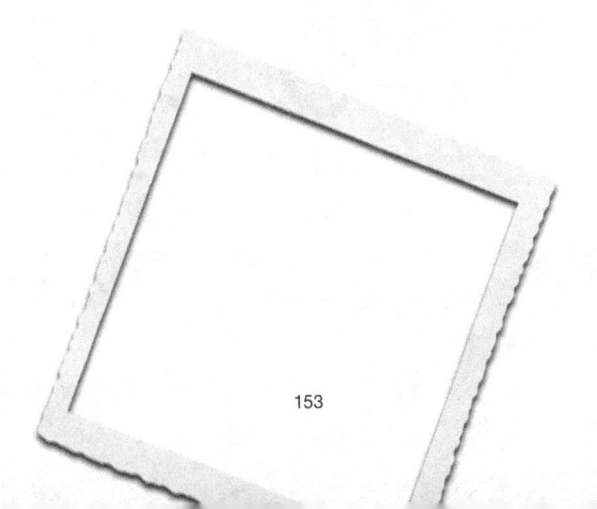

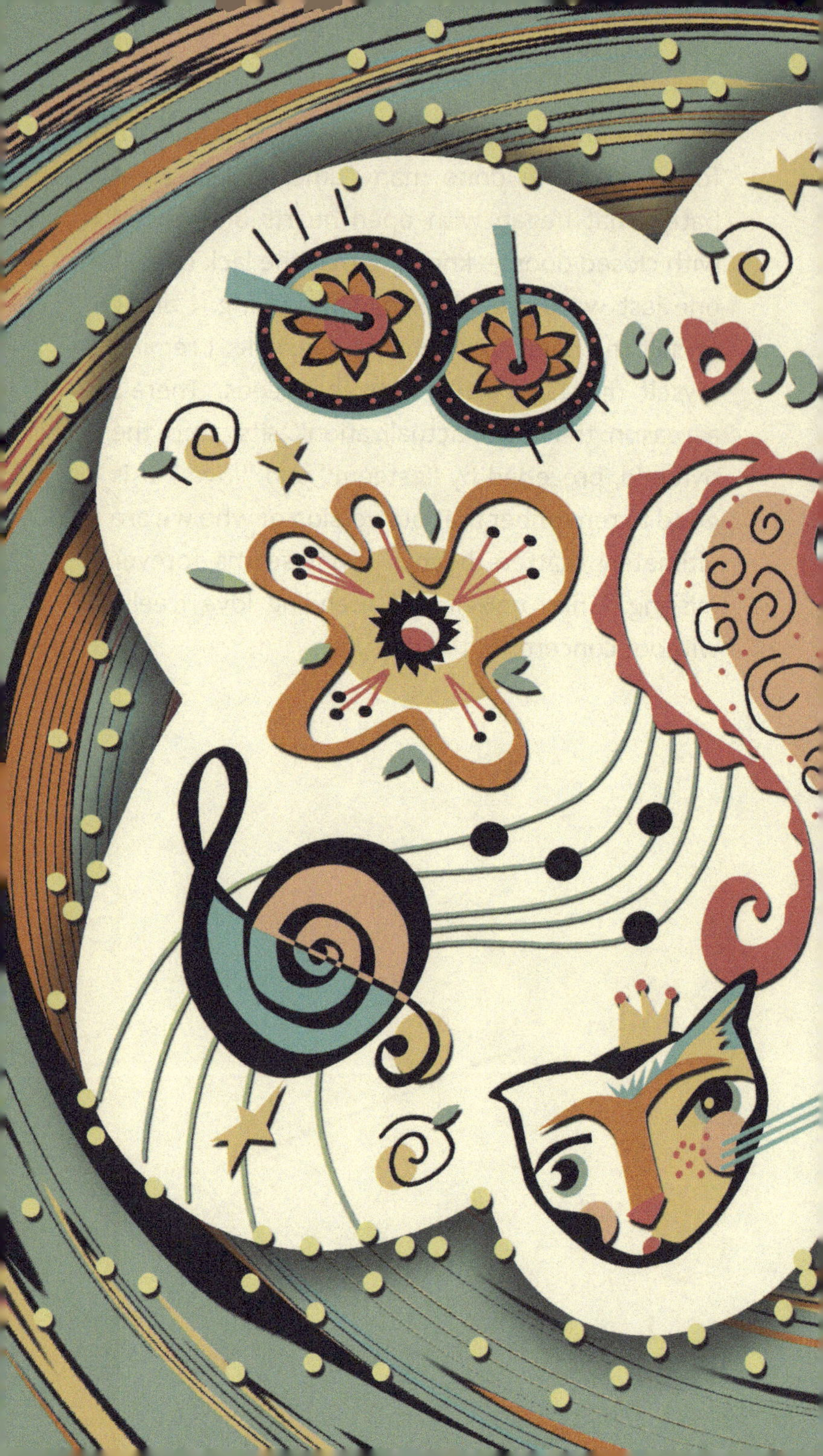

CLOUD THEORY

*I am breeze, silently brushing your face
so you remember I have been*

* * *

If I were to create a map of how to find me, it would lead you to discover me among the things and people I love. Lace-up your sneakers because I move fast and rarely in a straight line. Far from flighty, I am steadfast once centered around my nucleus. The center of all my journeys could be categorized as love. In fact, this essay could have been titled, *You Are What You Love*, but *Cloud Theory* is sexier.

I am, finally, circling what is in my heart. I have wised up, realizing that we are shaped by what we have and what we don't have. I feel gravity pulling people, places, and things of similar core values into my cloud. Let's rumble.

directions to where I live

SILENCE

For me, silence is felt as well as not heard. It rises early in the morning as the world wakes or in middle-nights when sleep can't find me. I cherish these noiseless wonders and their ability to arrive without a peep. They are, simultaneously, nothing and everything. There are too many soundless treasures to do more than list the ones I most adore. Your list will be different than mine, but my list may inspire you to hear silence differently.

WHAT SILENCE HOLDS

- Every thought at 2 AM
- Night sky lifting stars
- Morning coffee smelling of foreign lands
- A bird about to sing from a still tree
- A sleepless night that falls asleep
- Space between the end of a song and audience applause
- A poem about to be written
- Shadow of leaves crossing the wall as headlights pass through them in the dark
- Cool air hitting your skin

- A waking thought poised to escape, but you catch one beautiful line in half sleep, and give it life on the paper at your bedside
- When a person leaves your arms and takes up residence in your mind
- Loved ones who have passed sing a silent symphony in 30-part harmony on the inside of your chest
- Water echoes a last chance at your rising to to break its surface
- A hand rests on your leg, connecting past to present
- Waking alone, aware that silence is loud with conversation you can't quite hear
- A person struggling who is unable to make room for your help
- Plants providing oxygen
- Oxygen turning food into energy
- Warm laundry, unfolded, keeping each other company as they wrinkle
- Erasing words on paper that should never be written or said
- The lack of sound your thoughts make when forming a tear
- The split-second before a pencil hits the paper, poised in thought regarding how to say something that isn't nothing

MUSIC

Have you checked the grocery store aisle? That's me dancing through peppy tunes created to keep people moving and in the mood to spend. I sashay up to the yogurt cooler, having been asked (by the degree of my height) to reach for a blueberry yogurt needed by the young woman (lacking height) who has requested my help. Even I am surprised by how often this happens. I hope there's a Safeway store video that would attest to my gravitational pull. Please play this at my funeral as mourners smile and say, "Yep, that's her."

I am most interested in lyrics rather than instrumentation when I listen to music. In fact, I would be hard-pressed to name the instruments encountered on such musical journeys. The words sing high in triumph, low in despair, and hopeful in harmony, filling the space places that increase my heart's drumbeats.

When the music moves me, it moves me to dance with a regular foot frenzy and arm alarm. Most often, these are songs I've heard too many times to need reminding of the lyrics, but they are perfect for dancers bumping into each other, requiring a smiled apology. My attention falls on my nearest dancers as I attempt to follow their triumphant styles or grab a new move. My favorite dance partner is a professional belly dancer who can bring the funk down and dirty while her hands float wispy-delicate above her head, holding imaginary cymbals. Her hips figure eight ocean waves of perfection, her moves outwardly reveal the flaming embers of a slow burn. She closes her eyes, reaching for memories we will never see. A post-dance recap, however, shows that she has seen everything and everyone on the dance floor, on the stage, and in the audience. It is pure magic.

Next in the line of favorite dance partners is the one without rhythm or ease of movement who still chooses to hit the dance floor. Their seeming discomfort is endearing. These dancers are encouraged to move for the same reason I am—the beat, the feet, and the bodies joyfully clustered in the heat. Last notes cause dancers to hug their partners in gratitude or lay a hand on a stranger's arm, having shared a fullness that could not go without touching.

We've all experienced nostalgic songs that play our history. Perhaps a high school favorite that mix-tapes together a first kiss with the wrong person and a longing for the right person. Music soundtracks a memory, reminding us of hours of records played in small bedrooms. I often seek out songs written by friends and family members who sing their stories translucently for our traveling through. Passionate and sometimes painful, they close the gaps in time and loss. My late husband has written songs that my children still sing. The music and lyrics connect us in our varied feelings and healing, opening in petals—a white rose in every note.

ACCEPTANCE

My road to self-love has been a long one. At times, I wonder if it has no end. I've had my share of aha moments that leave no doubt I am human. During these times, enlightenment suggests, "Yes, I see this, and I have additional work to do." I hoist myself upon my own shoulders in triumph, looking forward to the goal ahead.

Self-acceptance arrives in baskets of lessons, having been sorted and decided upon. Some of these lessons get folded and placed in drawers while others get hung out in the breeze for a while, letting a clear day shake the dust from their long residence in one's self-doubt. I've learned to say "Thank you" for a compliment even when it seems utterly unbelievable. I hear small words of doubt like, "Why did I bring dates rolled in coconut to a party of 20-somethings, as a brief survey on the buffet table showcases chips, pretzels, Fritos, Cheetos, Doritos, and beer. "Too late," I think, feeling cold regret climb my veins while watching one party-goer try to palm off one of my rolled date creations—once bitten and twice shy—to a curious onlooker. "I think it's healthy," the young woman told her friend. I then shied from thinking that these youngsters probably thought I dressed as a hippie for this Halloween party (which I had not) instead of for Wednesday (which I had).

Years of feeling invisible and being named inadequate in one way or another have been, more or less so, put away. A few key images remain tattooed on my heart. They are the missed opportunities to ask for forgiveness from someone who can no longer forgive. I offer, in reciprocity, forgiveness to those who have wronged me and never apologized. They must be suffering, too. I recognize projection, fear, and retaliation as part of someone else's lack of acceptance for themselves. I know that I must accept them as they journey on their path. However, I can't always join them on that excursion, which causes me great sadness.

NATURE

Growing up in cities, I discovered the importance of nature in my middle years. The first time I felt an ocean grab my feet and claim me baptized anew was while seizing the opportunity to build a life on the West Coast. Since arriving in California, I've watched mountains turn from brown to green when fed by more rain than I've ever encountered, pouring for months. I'm getting used to the rainy season and hope to one day enjoy its urging to slow down, using it to write, have coffee with friends, and read. A downpour is beautiful to hear upon waking and while drifting off to sleep.

Redwood trees grow practically into the clouds on abundant sunny days and require our witness. Trails invite even novice hikers to walk slower, look deeper, and feel more. The forests are full of sounds in their silence. Deer families sometimes gather in the sunny spots between tree shadows, asking shoes to hush in reverent awe. We are part of them, as they are part of us.

Sunsets sing a glorious lullaby, and Coyote amble through my parking lot en route to the creek. Deer cross along roads that we have thoughtlessly laid in their path to find food once up the hill. Rumor has it that there's a Bobcat or two in the area, so I carry a whistle at night just in case I encounter one.

Birds are abundant outside my window. I live up a hill in a quiet neighborhood and have heard owls call to each other at twilight, while hoping that they are not as lonely as they sound. Flowers don't simply grow; they ignite in colors you may not have imagined possible. I stop to smell them, hoping to retain the memory of their sweet scent upon arriving home. Beaches laugh, and waves crash. Sand is everywhere after a trip to the ocean, and a shell often climbs into my pocket.

I admire a plant from my bed each morning occupying a small table on my balcony. It's the only live plant I maintain in a garden of its silk companions. I'm good at many things, but growing plants is not one of them. This plant, species unknown, is alone in the big world, but I recognize its good nature, having been gifted to me by a friend who wanted to extend her best wishes for happiness in my new home. I don't know much about plants in captivity, so I'm allowing this one to educate me. It may currently be telling me that it needs a larger pot. It looks like a size 9 in a size 7-1/2 shoe. We all require, at times, a new home to stretch out our roots.

REDEMPTION

Being aware that humans are fallible, I make room for those still working out their brand of mistreating themselves and others. If I am the target of their ire, I give them as many chances as possible to re-frame their position. The best-case scenario would include a beautifully crafted apology. I've met more than one person in my travels who never apologizes and seems quite proud of the whole damn situation. I wish I could show them that "I'm sorry" is another word for "freedom." I recognize their loneliness from the inside out and watch them in their solitary cloud. They can circle within my cloud because I've designated my forgiveness more important than their words, but I would be hard-pressed to join them in their cloud as we share different values. We each have our paths, and if welcomed, I hope to add value to another's journey, ever mindful of not depriving them of discovering happiness through earning it.

    I am firm regarding one point. In my particular cloud cluster, there is no space for apathy. When encountering such a person, I attempt to show, by example, why the world needs them to fill in the gaps between radiant sunrise and glorious sunset. I want them to consider their actions and inaction by metrics of how they may impact more than just themselves. I want them to listen for their name to be called and respond, "Yes."

LIGHT

I'm not always as successful as I hope to be in this short life, but I will continue to seek a good path for my soul before the long day ends. My life, maybe yours too, has been dark at times. Lives are messy, and outcomes are not guaranteed, but you can flip a switch to light another path in a more hopeful direction. I have engaged such a switch on multiple occasions, as life transitions make flexibility necessary. My switch may not be the same as yours, but what you desire to have as a human experience in our short time on earth may suggest keeping good faith in the world and investing in outcomes that benefit all of us.

I do not thrive in somber places or among angry words. I know those feelings and have left them behind with great resolve. I've learned to absorb their cruelty, to rest in the understanding of it, and to know that such behavior has harmed its owners more than me. It truly saddens me to let people go. I try not to do that too often.

I am trying to be a better, happier person and more open to how peace is defined. It's not always easy, but it is always worth it. My light dims from time to time. When it flickers or burns out briefly, I remind myself there can be grand learning in the dark. During these times, I rely on the light from others until I can, once again, find my own. My children are light; you are light. We are a corsage of fireflies clinging together on a balmy August night. We are the dashboard lights illuminated during phone calls from family and friends on their way home.

***

I am safely wrapped in this cloud I've worked hard to create, surrounded by warmth and happiness. I thank my family and friends for their understanding through difficult periods and I appreciate the great pleasure of their company. Our paths will continue to cross as we dart about our internal universes and light the way for others who feel lost. My way of life is not the only way to live, but I can attest that shifting from being a victim of occurrences to becoming responsible for my words and actions has improved my life. I laugh more often and enjoy sharing the best parts of living with those who hold my heart.

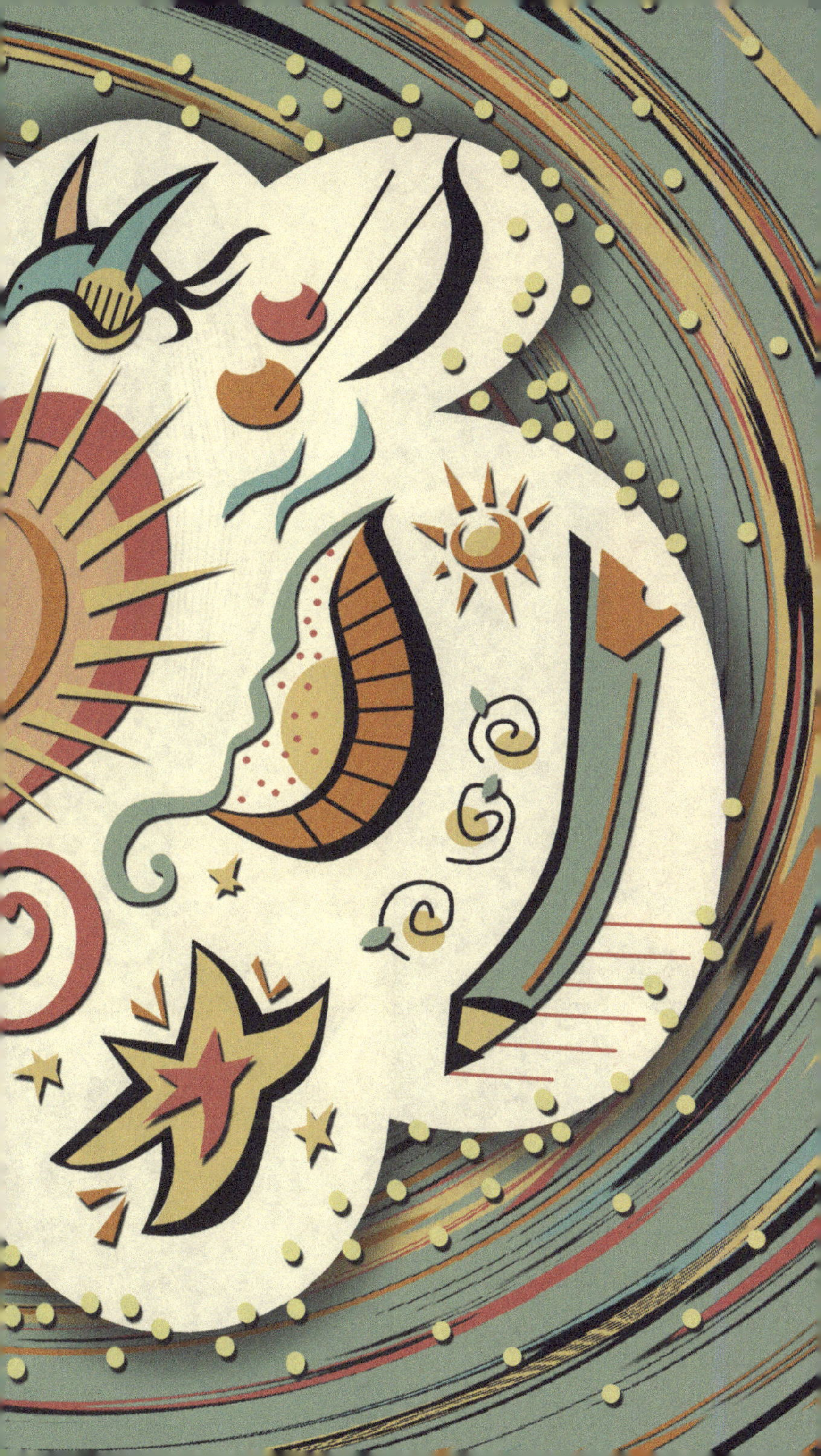

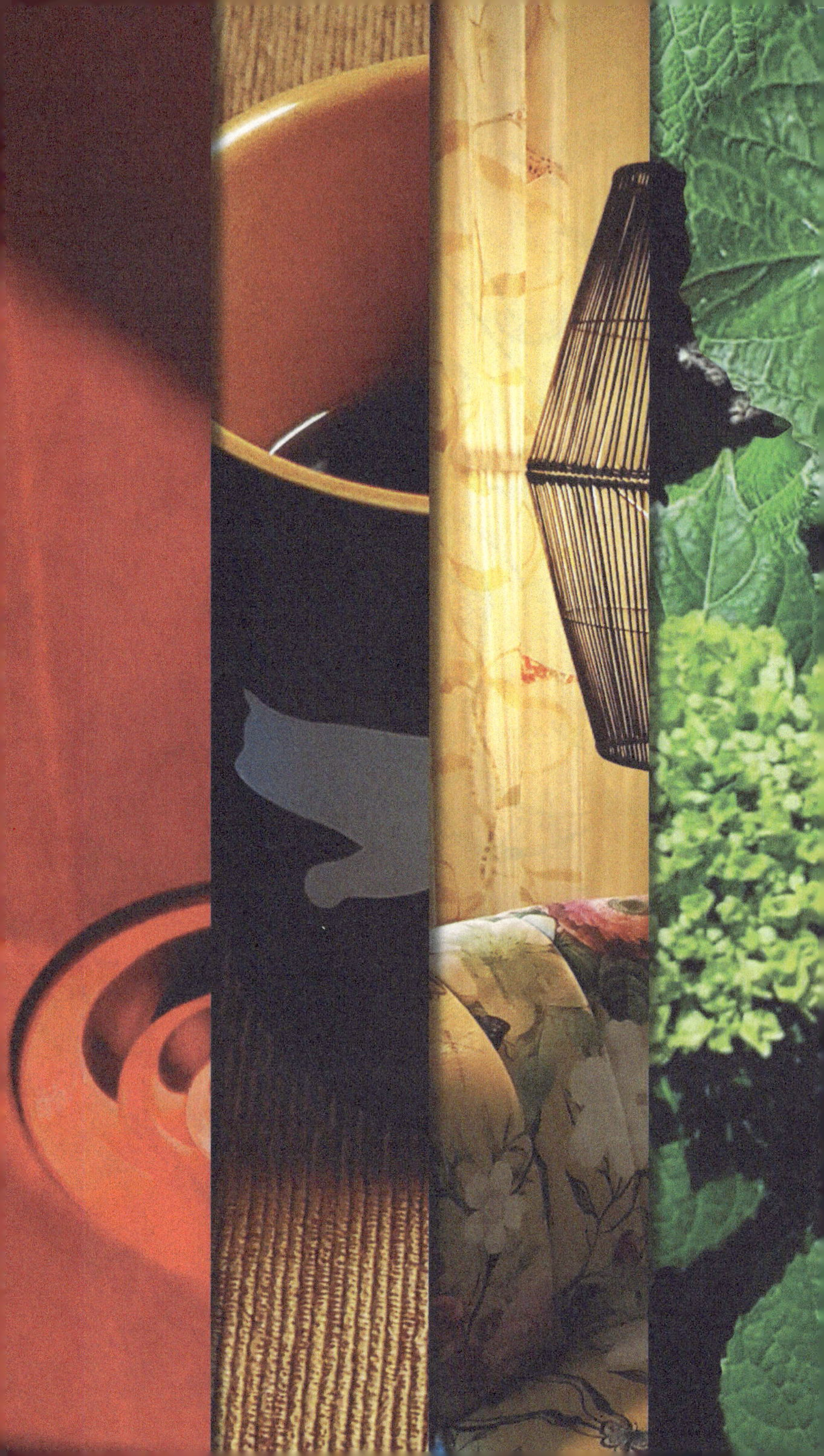

A RAINBOW OF GRATITUDE

we borrow our journeys between earth and sky
fill our souls with candles and prayer

* * *

I hope to live a colorful life and to see it reflected in the sunglasses of friends and family. I am thankful for beautiful outcomes often forged by hard times.

There are exceptions to every declaration. My children have greatly missed their father, the things he may have taught them, and the milestones he has missed. I may have traveled farther and with less difficulty if my husband had not so tragically passed at a young age. His practice of bringing me a single white rose on all occasions, and no occasion, leads me to proclaim that this flower, in its complete lack of color, represents the one person in my life for whom I am most grateful.

RED

His long wavelength demands attention
    warns of danger and signs that stop
A walking red flag of hot emotions
    in blood rising from neck to face
        a fiery mix of speedy heart and angry love

    names me the flame thrower

I thank the fear that moved me to place a hand
    on a doorknob
        a stairway rail
            a car-handled hopeful

I thank the quiet gardens in my town
Enthusiastic in their Hibiscus and Amaryllis
    for peace arriving in a song
        to sing from my kitchen window

ORANGE

Tasting life's sweetness
    stung on tongue
Exploding in sunshine
    that soothes my
    bent shoulders

I peel its skin in one long
    winding strip
Segment its pieces
Devour its ripe color
    in the shadow
    of a palm
    guarding my fair skin
    restoring my energy

I supervise the leaves

    falling too early
    to capture
    the fullness
    of their vibrancy

    twirl them like grief

Witness a flower
    named Bird
Unfurl its petals like
    wings for flying
    to Paradise
    on a hot day

YELLOW

The sun haunts straight arms, bent legs
    pulls cowardice from my pocket
Informs my growing in ways of fear
    in less than brilliant

The streak of it visible on unsturdy spines
    encountered in my over-deeds
    of uninspired repentance
Finding within this acre of yellow
    a closed dandelion
    bowed in a field of sunflowers

The day gathers balmy, rebirths a self
    that falls watering this folded weed
I carry home to place in a flawed and
    fluted crystal vase

GREEN

Rain thunders a heart
Dark with night
With flashes of light
Striking fear in
Downpours
That become out-pours

   I fall for days

Blown fierce by wind
Dashing hope in heaps
Having slid muddy
From mountainsides
To river flows

   of fresh calm

Beyond my shoes
Green breaks the earth

Fragile shoots grow
Determined in their
   quavering
Drink full a clear day
There is no bitterness

What was lost
Has returned to bathe
The forest in light
   in fetid moss
   in silent prayer

Treetops sparkle
Green with sunshine

Rain will wait
As I learn you in slices

   of ripe avocado

BLUE

I'm sorry for your despair on a day such as this
Breezed in lifted hats and patched jackets
    laughter riding the backs of tiny molecules
    bucking bronco style, one-handed

  so that you may

Leave heartache in your shoes on a rock
At the ocean's shell-swallowed edge
    feel it spray your face and fill your mouth
    as blackbirds mourn the sun's setting

  I ask you to

Make your sadness a trophy of abundance
Become the treasurer of this misfortune
    share its wealth with a friend
    that you both may become richer

INDIGO

The winter chill brings bold color
Having arrived carrying baskets
Of desert dust to Pacific a sunset

A gathering storm leaves bruises
Purple-blue on nameless clouds
Our words twilight disagreeably

I am blue calm, you purple frenzy
Each of us takes a bite of peach sky
As indigo drips off the world's edge

Leaving seconds of brilliant awe
Our voices discover hope hiding
In quiet breaths of astonishment

VIOLET

small in stature
tall in lovely
stemmed for
young wonder
to gather

but for your
dazzling color
you may have been
stepped on
or overlooked
in forest or clearing

you might not have
worn this royal robe
to warm our
older years
as we remember
being small
preferring to shrink

in the company
of wild people
and flowers

feral violets
may find themselves
blue-ribboned
together and
placed in water
for a weary mother's
arrival home from
an unpleasant day
at a job she hates

thank you violets
for promise in your
delicate petals
always open
flashing neon
your welcome

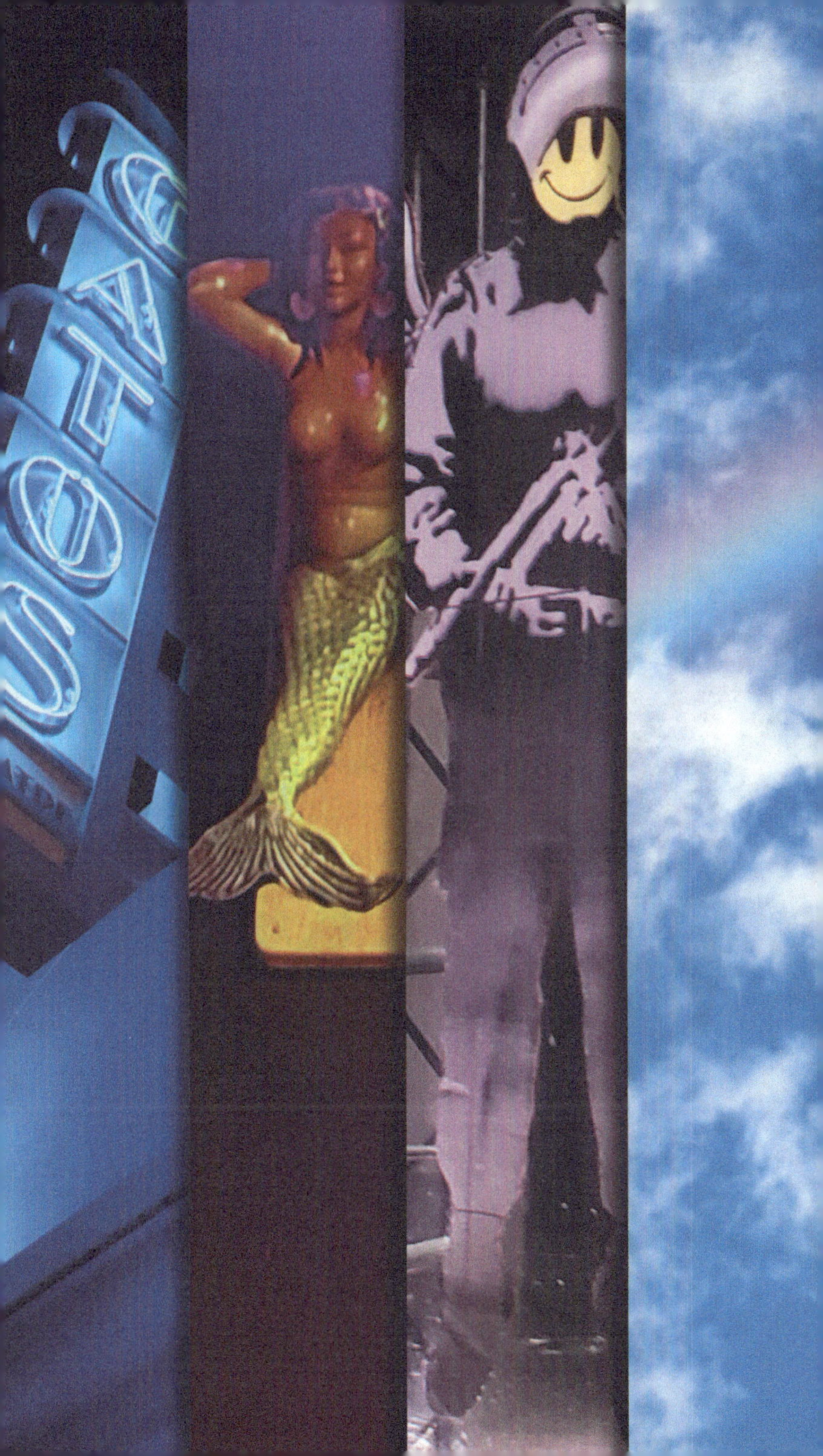

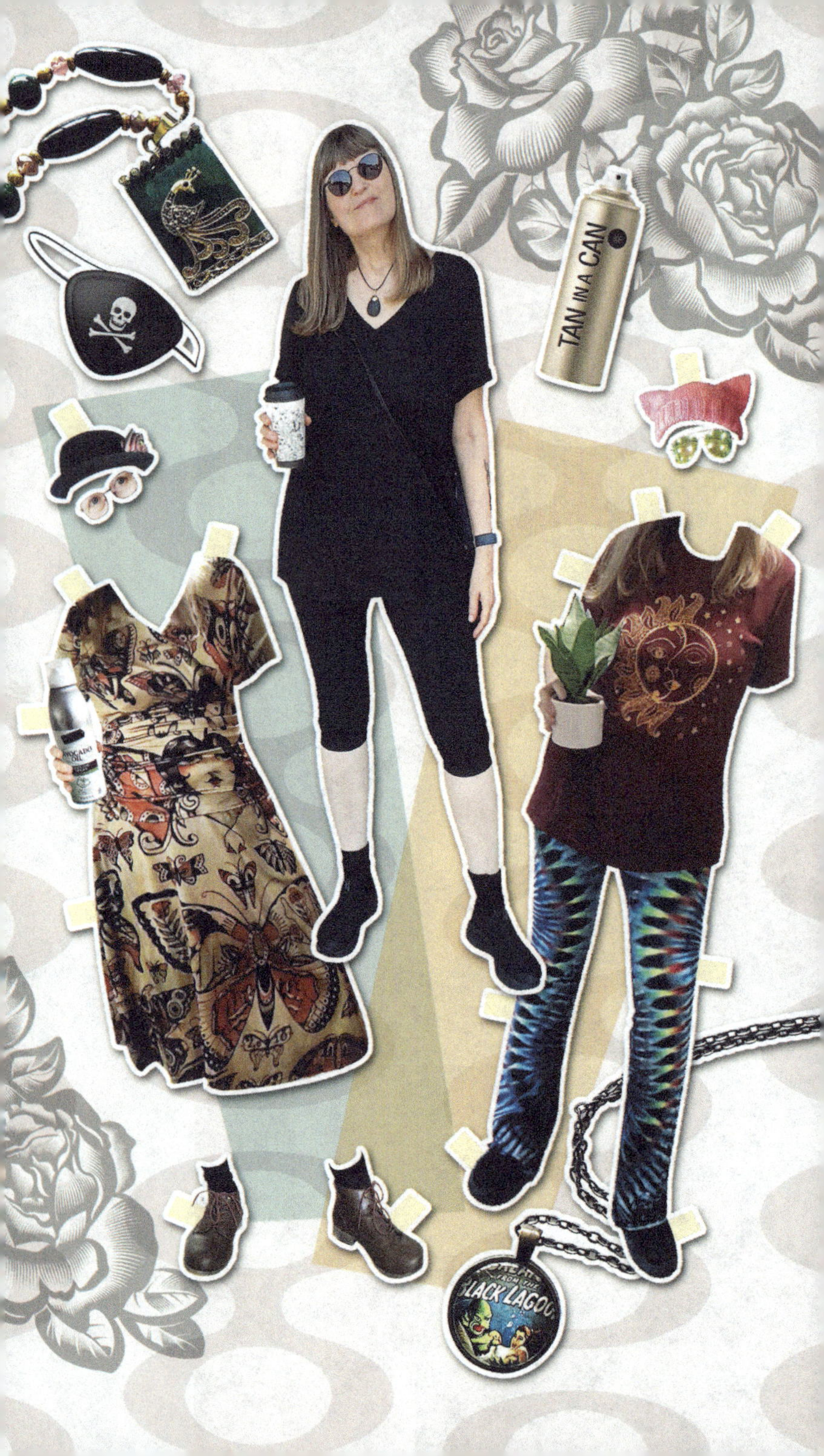
TAN IN A CAN

BECOMING A PIECE OF WORK

drowned in my willingness to remain anonymous
among the spillers of grace
I reach for anything that isn't nothing

* * *

Now that I had a new life on a new coast, my self-conscious bias prompted me to review the clothes in my closet. I used to be basic black, a dark figure against every bright background. Flowers in sidewalk gardens and geometrics covering chairs in the beautiful homes of friends wrapped my anonymity. I asked myself, "Why has this been true for most of my adult years, and why is it not true now?" Something had changed me, or someone had pulled too hard on a thread that could have been my undoing.

It was summer in a new home state. I remembered that I was beautiful and funny and could still be those things in brilliant tie-dye and mismatched patterns, my fashion imprint conforming to my body in non-conformity. Note to self: This is California; I could disappear by standing out. I no longer stood against the world but stood with it as an additional layer of snazzy. I was a closet wide open.

You, too, can become your own piece of work. Not necessarily the flashy kind, but the stylish, suited, beige, gowned, bow-tied, hatted, or shorts-wearing in a snowstorm kind. As the Avett Brothers (my favorite band and ceaseless crush) sing in their song *Head Full of Doubt,* "Decide what to be and go be it."

***

BECOME A PIECE OF WORK

You need not be conflated with any prior circumstances that may have caused your entire existence to be imprisoned by the things of life. You have earned the right to be exactly who you are. Now is always a good time to begin. Once you've hopped the fence, you'll see yourself from the other side. You are free.

IF YOU FIND YOURSELF UNRAVELING

How does one exist in a world that spins around while they are spinning in circles? Re-spool. Unwind as necessary to find the knot that disallowed your unique spin on life. Believe that you know what's best for you and that whoever tried to snag, knot, or break your phenomenal revolution was misguided. Look at a picture from your childhood and understand that the fresh little human, dressed in stiff clothes and hard shoes, was someone else's idea of perfection. Also, realize that "perfection" is a relative (and therefore imperfect) term.

SHODDY CRAFTSMANSHIP

Please recognize that people who think it's okay to hurt you do so because they have not yet defined who they want to be. Perhaps they are angry that others are "getting all of the breaks," or they believe they "deserve better than so-and-so," or that they are "smarter than everyone else." These folks become their own enemy and will shrink behind their own line of defense. We can try to tell them they are remarkable without the constant bullshit, but we must realize they may not be ready to believe it. Put a little distance between you and them

OFF THE RACK

Stop torturing yourself by not recognizing the woven magic of your existence. Your childhood, your status, your job ... none of it defines you. You made it to this point no matter what the world or cast of characters in your orbit has led you to believe about yourself. Stretch beyond your limit of comfort. Take a few chances. Learn something new. You may find people who revolve around the same heart as you do.

IMPECCABLE QUALITY

When you meet someone you admire, it's perfectly fine to emulate their best qualities until they become yours, too. People of quality are pleased to be your guide to discovery and will love you for loving them.

HAND SEWN

Of the piecework I most admire are people who have had to work the hardest to stitch themselves together after a lifetime of trauma. Their bravery is often worn on the sleeves of their shirts. They have learned to be kind due to unkind treatment toward them. Instead of becoming hardened, they've become soft by triple washing. They have managed to sew a new life for themselves and their families. They are the most exciting mosaic of people and places who, unable to forget their past tragedies, still choose to sew colorful patches over their missing parts using the most delicate embroidery. Wrap them in your arms. You will become a better person for it.

***

I met my reflection the other day. I was looking in a shop window where sophisticated mannequins wore tailored dresses. Superimposed on their magnificence, I encountered my righteous soul, whom I'd lost for a long time. I claimed victory and peace in the same slow breath. I move forward, content in knowing that everything looks different once you've crossed enough borders. I am rewoven smarter, kinder, funnier, and will be the piece of work in every quilt that may not quite fit. I like that.

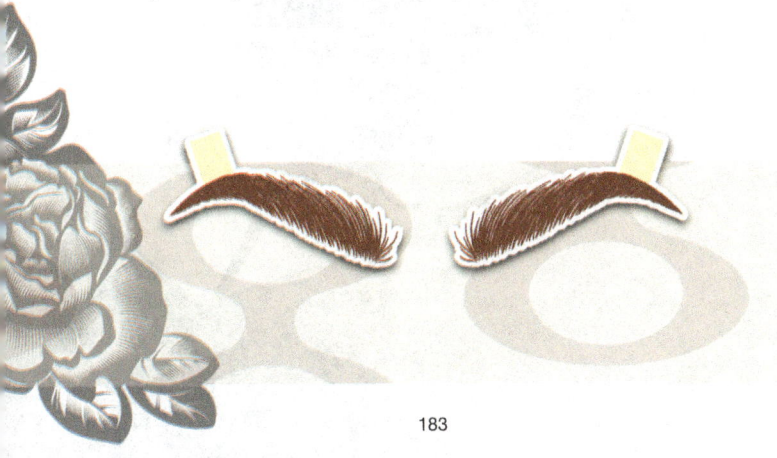

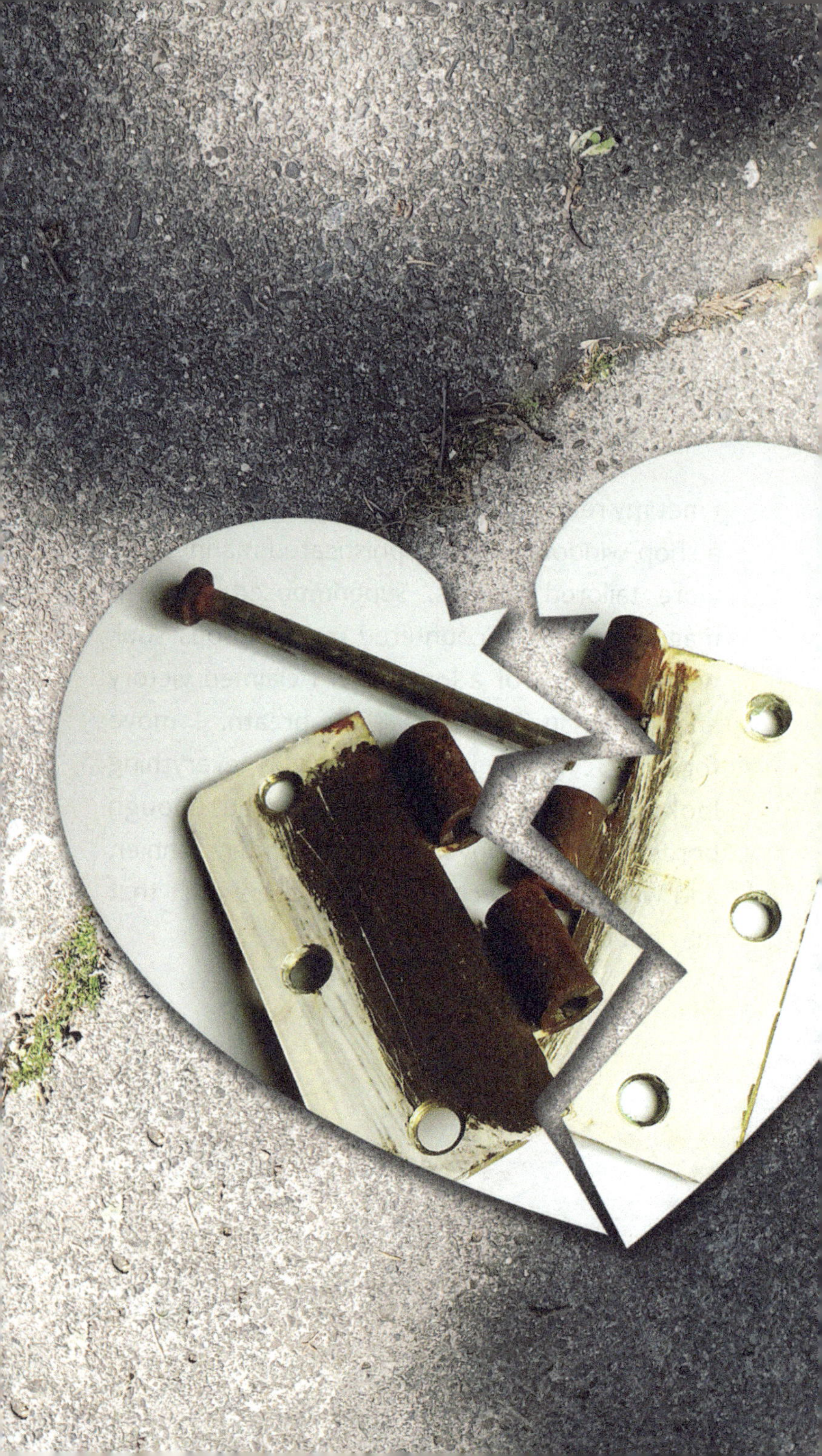

TRUST ME, I'M A DOCTOR

ACCIDENT PRONE

*what if I told you that I am solid on this day
clear-eyed and careful, prepared to
fall down in important ways*

* * *

I've fallen so often that a photograph of myself in an arm brace and a half-leg boot causes me to speculate which spectacular spill this might have been. In other photos, verdigris bruises, a bloodied big toe (minus half of a toenail), and a bright red scrape all serve to demonstrate how quickly a step-up can become a fall-down.

I've sprained this and that, twisted joints hither and yon, been stitched together now and then, but have never broken a bone. I've "rearranged" those bones and taped them to a neighboring appendage to cocoon in motionless pupation while hoping for an early spring.

Some photos warn the other jammed finger or out-of-whack shoulder to straighten up. "Don't forget that handrails are for holding, and cotton socks on hardwood floors may become lethal weapons."

I once was able to splat on concrete, finish the job, pick up the kids, make dinner, and go to the park, only later to discover the dry, bloodied gash on one leg as it slips into a pajama bottom to await cleanup the following morning. However, it's been a while since I've taken any significant spills. I've grown older and more cautious. The splints, braces, elastic bandages, and ice packs in my closet remain primarily ignored as I reach for a new cream guaranteed to smooth out wrinkles, the current catastrophic event. I do, occasionally, acknowledge their existence. Say, "Thanks for the support, my lonely gadgets. I love you, but I hope to never again need you."

I grow vitamin-ed and resilient in body and mind. The heart, however, often needs tending. When it fractures, I find myself wrapping it in acceptable words from a good friend. I protect that smooth muscle and allow its four chambers to echo a concerto that reverberates in my chest, sings my life, and waits for applause.

This older heart often takes longer to heal than it did as a young woman. Don't forget that hands are for holding I think as I call a father, a brother, a son, a daughter. I lay low and check my email more times than necessary in case there may be an apology or acknowledgment of a mistake. Instead, I find a cascade of scrolling email titles that read like a menu for old age. "Well, I guess this is goodbye, Cheryl," from Hot Topic online. "10 seconds to lose 54 lbs." "Fight aging odor" or simply "Farting."

I've built an adequate First Aid Kit over the years, filling it with all I need to fix what is broken or requires forgiveness. A floral box, with gold hinges and a latch, holds dried petals from a bouquet that remembers how we bloom and then drop sorrowfully as time demands. A yellowed letter confesses first love, a ring from my husband, and two sets of tiny baby footprints. A Godzilla cigarette lighter no longer "breathes" fire when its scales are pressed. I shuffle the few photos, including a 2-year-old me standing in front of my grandmother's house and shielding my eyes from the sun. There are pins, homemade gifts, a tie, and a pair of glasses. This box, this lifetime of healing, awaits my rescue from every high falling.

It has been in these accidental moments that I've accidentally discovered that I love myself. It was surprising to learn who I am and be enamored of that person who, ironically, has always been who I have always been. Some moderation in tone and kindness, of course, as becoming older reminds us how unnecessary rude behavior is. And I'm not bragging, but I can dance. Not the lovely partnered flow, which I sorely do wish for, but a monkey flailing of sorts. What may look like a pre-fall attempt to balance a crooked life is actually the splendor of a purposeful wiggling of arms and legs. I dance, chicken-like, squabbling my way through a barnyard brawl. I wind up like a windmill on fire, displaying a whipping, dipping, and scooting that one may misconstrue as an attempt to remain upright—of course, it is. Still, against this "odd" of my creation, I'm convinced I am invisible whether the dance floor is crowded or empty. I like it this way.

These days, I choose my words as cautiously as my steps (though sometimes I curse like a crabby old man ... as a treat). Most often, however, my words live in my deeds. I make mistakes, but I try to fix them immediately. I embrace melancholy for its healing properties. I leave people whole when I leave them. Forgive.

Encourage. Say "Thank you" for all that has led me to this surprising place of here and now.

A favorite of the scars I carry, visible and invisible, is the dent in my chin. It was cracked open while ice-skating on the lagoon. Tripping on the ice, I face-planted that 12-year-old chin on a sharp rock sticking up through the ice. The resulting "cleft" is worthy of Kirk Douglas.

I admire my hands, each bearing a like-sized scar. Lefty boasts a clean 6-stitcher made by an X-Acto knife prank perpetrated by a genuine "cut-up" when I worked in the art department at American Express. Righty enjoys a lumpy scar bestowed by the ragged edge of a glass that I was washing, having broken it as I twisted my sponge inside it.

The real scars, the ones that even close observers cannot see, are still capable of haunting in surprise-pain avalanches.

Scars that love in their lessons have ceased to be painful. They can still knock me off my feet but never let me fall. More often, they pool in grateful memories that live in the upturned corner of my half-smile.

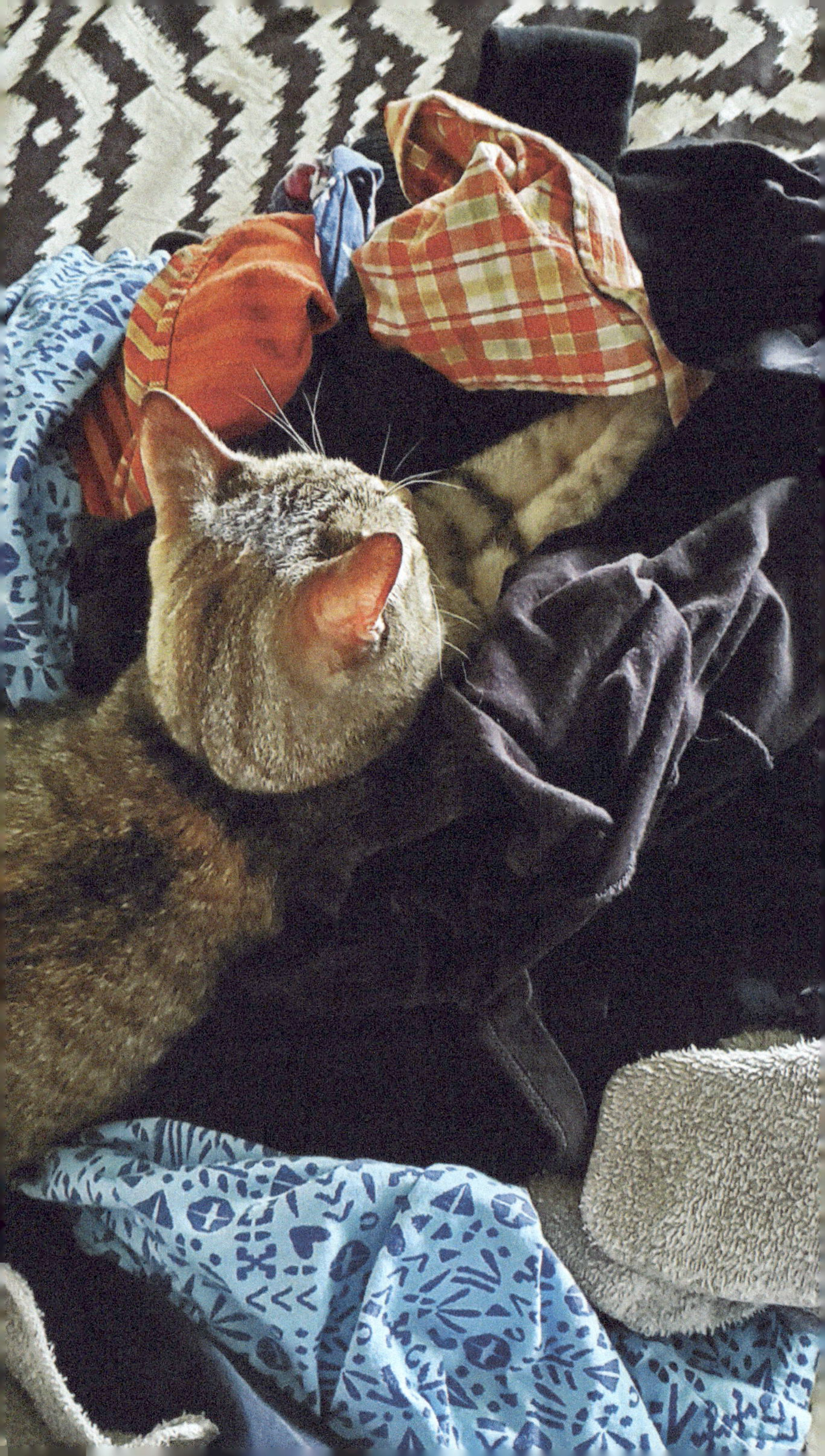

BUILDING HOUSES

*my waking found sunlight from un-shuttered
windows bathing the floor in rectangles
their warm stepping-stones to steal the chill
from bare feet*

* * *

I moved into my current and beautiful apartment eight months ago. This second-floor wonder has windows across the living room and bedroom walls, with a door in each room to step out onto a narrow balcony. Out beyond those windows, a pink wall of Oleander had obscured the houses on the next street. It felt as though only I existed in this world-turned-tree house. I slept with the "wall" open during my first night in my new home. I woke to buzz saws and jackhammers early the next day. Big trucks rolled in with needed material; their backup beeping forced the cat under the bed and me from my pillow. Workmen shouted to each other, hoping to be heard above the jangle of chaos.

It wasn't until the Oleander withered that I saw the house being built on the other side of my personal forest. It continues to be a work in progress, but most of the racket has now moved to the inside of the home and is a bit muffled. I imagine what type of kitchen the new owners chose and what flooring defines them. Did the cabinets need to be set lower to accommodate their stature? Is it a first home or last? Is there space enough for household members to brand themselves in a choice of bedspreads and pillows? I can't wait to see who moves in, believing them so lucky to have constructed their home on the side of a hill with a mountain view. I hope they will be happy with how they have built themselves.

* * *

Those of us who have lived in San Jose, California, are more likely than not to have brought visiting guests to tour the Winchester Mystery House. The ghosts of those murdered by the "Gun that Won the West" plagued poor Sarah Winchester, heir to the Winchester Rifle fortune. A psychic, the story continues, told Sarah that the ghosts would not harm her if construction on the house were never to stop. And so it continued from 1886-1922. Touring this 24,000-square-foot structure is a study in madness. Most of the 47 stairways and fireplaces do not function. I found it unsettling to see most stairways end when they reached the ceiling. Most of the 2,000 doors opened to the walls behind them (the tiny doors made my stomach uneasy). I could feel the inside of poor Sarah on full display, her mind only resting easier by the sound of constant banging.

Over my lifetime, I have met people who have used their homes in perplexing ways, yet once I got to know them better, they make perfect sense. Some live in museums that mark their travels and storied accomplishments. Their lives unfold in artifacts or extraordinary achievements, sharing this bloom with their many friends. My version of this is more modest. I keep scrapbooks, letters, and drawings from my children. I photograph people and places that tell my story in images small enough to pack for the next move. These things are as treasured as if discovered on an archaeological dig. Uncovered and brushed of dust by me, they have found a home in my body.

Some people lock their doors from the

outside but not from the inside. Others leave their doors wide open when they leave, knowing that nothing inside their house is as valuable as what they carry with them. Random burglars, or even known friends, will never take what forever belongs to these folks. In a small way, I may own this sense of self. I protect my space externally and internally from those who have no need for buried treasure.

> I know a man who refuses to fix a dripping faucet because the sound of water hitting porcelain reminds him of who and where he is.
>
> •
>
> I know a woman whose leaky roof prevents her from remembering her children's names.
>
> •
>
> I know a man who has built tall walls with no doorway to allow exit or entry.
>
> •
>
> I know a woman who tears apart and then rebuilds every bit of her house because she still has not decided who she is.

> I know a man who sweeps debris into corners rather than relying on dustpan pick-up and removal. He builds a maze of strange things he's collected. He seems comfortable among what some would consider garbage.
>
> I know of another man who surrounds himself with the trappings of wealth, including a solid gold toilet. Even he must be aware that the only thing puffing up that 2XL blue suit and red tie is an over-inflated ego and a lot of hot air. He must know, I believe, that his life is of no value to anyone—including himself.

I am more a decorator than a builder, having only once lived in a house I owned. I have moved 18 times so far, more often by circumstance than choice. I decorated each new apartment according to what I felt at the time. During times of pain, my walls may wait patiently for healing or for the next move to a happier place and time.

Today, I fill the rooms with inexpensive and uncomfortable furniture because I don't know how long I'll be here, and such large items don't usually move with me. I curtain to soften my view from the windows. I fold a chair on the balcony and sit outside to feel the day. I turn on too many lamps because sometimes the lights must stay lit to see clearly.

Nothing in my home looks like it belongs with anything else, and yet it feels harmonious with birds and robots, a geometric pillow snuggled up to one with a vintage floral pattern. I don't know if I'll ever stop moving or find a final home. It would be nice to have enough room for the family at Christmas.

* * *

I find that house cleaning starts with necessity but ends with finding something that has long been missing. I have to spend several minutes looking at it before finally dusting it and putting it back on the shelf from which it fell. Maybe it was something small that a friend had given me 40 years ago. Or it may have been a ticket for some unknown violation, which has become an obsolete relic of the past.

I was searching my closet recently. I was trying to find a photograph that I knew I had kept. I could not find it, but I discovered a story my son had written about the Christmas he spent at his grandparents' house and leaving that house without his father. Don had passed in the middle of the night. A blood clot from Cellulitis in his leg had stopped his big, beautiful heart from beating. With my two very young children, I returned to the only house that I would ever, to this day, call home. It was now as empty as our house would forever feel without my husband, their father. We began rebuilding because this is what we always do.

* * *

Every day, I grow my house stronger and wiser. Some of us put up fences. Others water the grass and plant perfect flowers, opening their windows to view how the world sees them. We patch the cracks and replace broken glass that keeps us from seeing the real world. Depending on where we live, we may have the added task of protecting ourselves from rivers that overflow and the earth that shifts beneath our feet.

At my new apartment, I continue to receive mail addressed to former residents. The letters belong to Jonathan, Ashley, Celia, and Roger—a cast of characters who once lived in my rooms before moving on. I hope they've found what they were searching for. I hope that these misdirected messages, having been returned "not at this address," will eventually find them and that my invisible roommates will not have lost themselves.

I found a tiny mushroom growing in my bathroom sink this morning. I plucked it from the drain with a tissue. It had no root to speak of, just a little extra width at the base of its stem. It was determined to grow big with little support. I understood this and felt immediate remorse at its destruction, wishing I'd planted it in a teacup and moved it to its own shady home on my balcony.

While here, I will remind myself that every door has a key, and knowing when to use it is essential—to keep safe or to open wide to new adventures. Each threshold I cross is an opportunity to carry in suitcases of heartache or leave the baggage outside and enter a new life that smells of apples baking. There is always a choice.

The door inside my heart is open to those who are kind and know how to hold the door for others. There will always be plenty of space here because I continue to grow. Come in. I have a TV and burritos.

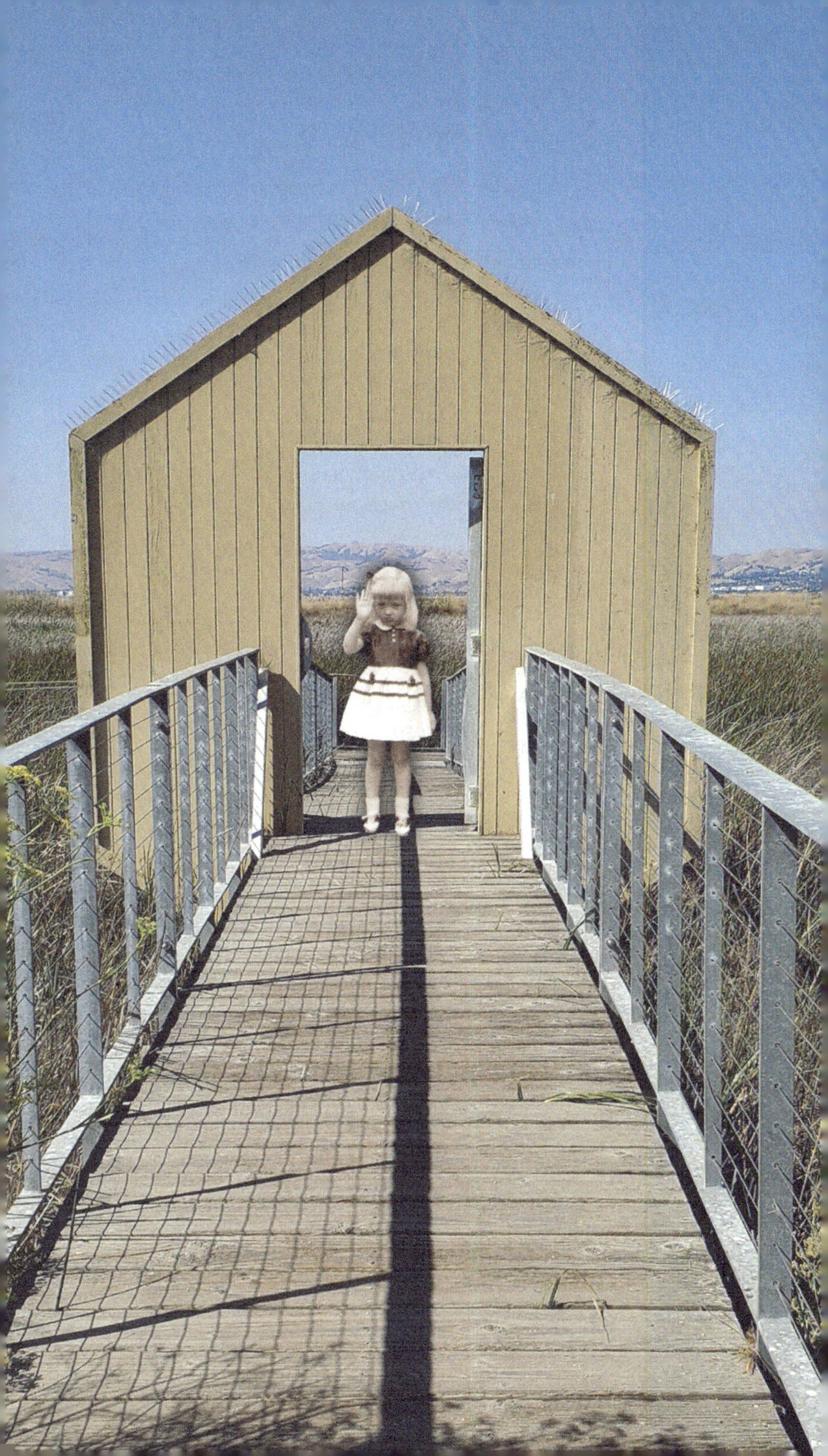

ACKNOWLEDGMENTS

Pins above the title of each essay
were collected by Don Brody

Photographs throughout are either by myself,
or used by permission from:
Amy Biggers
Judy Brody
Molly Brody
Perry Brody
Rae Welch
William Whitehurst
Roy Yokelson

Some collages include images purchased
from iStock Photo

Special thanks to
Chris Carrington Winters
for reading pages, and providing ideas
and inspiration

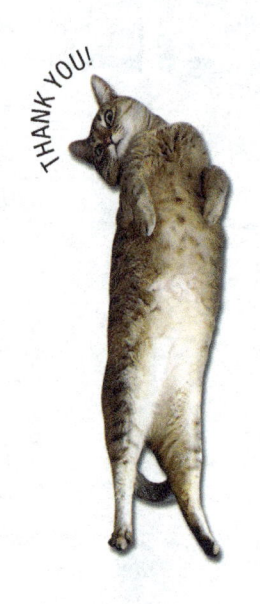

CHERYL WELCH

*Artist, Writer, and Poet
Mother and Friend
Working hard to become an all-around
Good Egg*

* * *

THRIVING SOMETIMES LOOKS LIKE STANDING STILL

REFERENCE LIST

"Why are so many dead invasive fish washing up on Lake Michigan beaches?" Michigan Public, Lester Graham, 22, June 2022 at 7:43 PM EDT. Accessed April 8, 2024, https://www.michiganpublic.org/environment-climate-change/2022-06-22/why-are-so-many-dead-invasive-fish-washing-up-on-lake-michigan-beaches

•

"United States lightship Frying Pan," Wikipedia, Wikimedia Foundation, 23 August 2023. Accessed April 20, 2024, https://en.m.wikipedia.org/wiki/United_States_lightship_Frying_Pan_(LV-115)

•

Winchester Mystery House Website Accessed April 24, 2024, https://winchestermysteryhouse.com/

•

"Doctor McCoy's Legendary Lines," Jay Stobie, 20 January 2023. Accessed May 28, 2024, https://www.startrek.com/news/doctor-mccoys-legendary-lines

•

"10 Spock Quotes to Remember Leonard Nimoy," The Hollywood Reporter Staff, 27 February 2015. Accessed May 28, 2024, https://www.hollywoodreporter.com/movies/movie-news/star-trek-quotes-leonard-nimoy-778305/

Made in the USA
Monee, IL
27 June 2024

60737568R00115